The GREATEST FIGHT

ORIGINALLY PRESENTED BY CHARLES SPURGEON
AT A CONFERENCE AT THE PASTOR'S COLLEGE.

The
GREATEST
FIGHT

Spurgeon's Urgent Message for
Pastors, Teachers, and Evangelists

Charles H. Spurgeon

We love hearing from our readers. Please contact us at www.anekopress.com/questions-comments with any questions, comments, or suggestions.

The Greatest Fight – Charles H. Spurgeon
Revised Edition Copyright © 2018
First edition published 1891

Scripture quotations are taken from the Jubilee Bible, copyright © 2000, 2001, 2010, 2013 by Life Sentence Publishing, Inc. Used by permission of Life Sentence Publishing, Inc., Abbotsford, Wisconsin. All rights reserved.

Cover Design: Natalia Hawthorne, BookCoverLabs.com

eBook Icon: Icons Vector/Shutterstock

Editors: Michelle Rayburn, M.A. and Ruth Zetek

Printed in the United States of America

Aneko Press – *Our Readers Matter*[TM]

www.anekopress.com

Aneko Press, Life Sentence Publishing, and our logos are trademarks of
Life Sentence Publishing, Inc.
203 E. Birch Street
P.O. Box 652
Abbotsford, WI 54405

RELIGION / Christian Ministry / General

Paperback ISBN: 978-1-62245-504-1

eBook ISBN: 978-1-62245-505-8

10   9   8   7   6   5   4   3   2

Available where books are sold

Contents

Editor's Foreword..IX

Ch. 1: Our Fight 1

Ch. 2: Our Armory 7

Ch. 3: Our Army 49

Ch. 4: Our Strength...65

Conclusion 85

Charles Spurgeon – A Brief Biography 87

Editor's Foreword

It was only six years after he came to Christ in 1850 at the age of sixteen that Charles Haddon Spurgeon founded Spurgeon's College. As a gifted preacher and communicator himself, he wanted to train others who would bring the gospel to the world. Spurgeon preached nearly thirty-six hundred sermons in his lifetime, before his death in 1892.

This is a modern adaptation of the final inaugural address delivered by Spurgeon at the College Conference, a gathering of pastors at Spurgeon's College in April 1891. This book is an encouragement to all believers who are warriors in the crusade against error and sin. It was published after his death and has continued to be a resource and inspiration for more than 125 years.

This speech was given to pastors, but the message is relevant to all who are part of the army of the Lord. Whether one is a minister, Bible teacher, small group leader, workplace evangelist, or any ministry leader, there is something to be gained from Spurgeon's convictions. There is no doubt that he was firm in his theology and not the least bit afraid of being unpopular for speaking truth.

Although some hold a great appreciation for this and other Spurgeon sermons, others may have missed his timely message as they struggled to work through sentences crafted in Old English that have been replaced by a new set of semantics in our present century. The outdated expressions might have masked a message that is in no way outdated.

We have revised *The Greatest Fight in the World* by replacing the terminology from the 1800s with language that modern readers would understand, while keeping the heart of the message unchanged. We have worked to retain the poetic way in which Spurgeon spoke wherever possible so that we wouldn't erase his DNA from the original text.

Every line and phrase has been carefully studied and words compared to those in the Oxford English Dictionary to compare archaic uses of many words that are no longer used in the same way as they once were.

Biographical notes have been added where possible, which will help readers identify the specific people whom Spurgeon addressed in the sermon. This information will provide the curious readers with a starting point, should they wish to complement their reading with further research. We have used the *Jubilee Bible* to update the references from Scripture used throughout the book.

It is our sincere hope that by updating this book, it will open doors for more people to experience the great preacher Charles Haddon Spurgeon. This essay will give readers a glimpse into the development of the Christian church in the late 1800s, and many will find the themes to be true still today.

Chapter 1

Our Fight

May all the prayers which have already been offered up be answered abundantly and speedily! May more of this kind of pleading follow the prayers in which we have already united! The most memorable part of past conferences has been the holy concert of believing prayer, and I trust we are not falling off in that respect, but growing even more fervent and prevalent in intercession. On his knees, the believer is invincible.

I have been greatly concerned about this address for many months before the opportunity to speak came. I assure you, this speech is born out of many prayers. I would like to be able to speak well on such a worthy occasion, where the best delivery would be expected. But I desire to be, as our brother's prayer has put it, absolutely in the Lord's hands in this matter, as well as in every other. I would be willing to speak with stammering tongue if God's purpose could be more fully presented. I would even gladly lose all power of speech if, by being starved for human words, you might have your hunger satisfied on the spiritual meat which is found alone in Him, who is the incarnate Word of God.

That said, I say to you, as speakers, that I am persuaded we should carefully prepare ourselves, and we should try to do our very best in our great Master's service.

I think I have read that when a handful of lion-like Greeks blocked the advance of the Persians, a spy, who came to see what they were doing, went back and told the king they were poor creatures, because they were occupied with combing their hair. The king saw things clearly when he learned that those who could adjust their hair before battle had set a great value on their heads, and therefore would not bow them to a coward's death.

If we are careful to use our best language when proclaiming eternal truths, we will lead our opponents to assume we are even more careful of the doctrines themselves. We must not be untidy soldiers when a great fight is before us, for that would look like hopelessness.

We advance into the battle against false doctrine, worldliness, and sin, without a fear regarding the ultimate issue. Therefore, our talk should not be that of untidy passion, but of well-considered principle. We should not be slovenly, since we seek to be triumphant. Do your work well at this time, so all people may understand you will not be driven from it.

The Persian, on another occasion when he saw a handful of warriors advancing, said, "That little handful of men! Surely, they cannot mean fighting!"

But one who stood nearby said, "Yes, they do, for they have polished their shields and shined their armor."

Be assured, people mean business when they are not willing to be rushed into a fight. It was customary among the Greeks, when they had a bloody day before them, to show the stern joy of warriors by being well dressed.

I think, brothers, that when we have great work to do for Christ, and are intentional about it, we will not go to the pulpit or the platform to say the first thing that comes to the lip.

We are feeble, but the Lord our God is mighty, and the battle is the Lord's, rather than ours.

If we speak for Jesus, we ought to speak at our best, although even then, men are not conquered by the glitter of shields, nor by the smoothness of a warrior's hair, but a higher power is needed to cut through armor.

To the God of armies, I look up. May He defend what is right! But I do not advance to the front with careless steps; neither do I have any doubt. We are feeble, but the Lord our God is mighty, and the battle is the Lord's, rather than ours.

I have only one fear, to a certain degree. I am anxious that my deep sense of responsibility may not lessen my efficiency. A man may feel he ought to do so well that, for that very reason, he may not do as well as he could. An overpowering feeling of responsibility may lead to paralysis.

I once recommended a young clerk to a bank, and his friends gave him strict instructions to be very accurate with his arithmetic. He thought about this advice often, to the point of obsession. He became so extremely careful that he grew nervous, and where he had been accurate before, his anxiety caused him to make mistake after mistake, until he left his job. It is possible to be so anxious about how you will speak and what you will speak on that your delivery becomes forced and stiff, and you forget the very points which you meant to make most prominent.

Brothers, I am telling some of my private thoughts to you, because we are alike in our calling, and because we have the same experiences. It does us good to know we have camaraderie. Those of us who lead have the same weaknesses and troubles as those who follow. We must prepare, but we must also trust in Him – the One without whom nothing begins, continues, or ends right.

I have this comfort: even if I do not speak adequately on my subject, the topic itself will speak to you. There is something to be said for even starting an appropriate subject. If a man speaks well on a subject that has no practical importance, it isn't good that he should have spoken at all.

As someone once said, "It is idle to speak much to the point upon a matter which itself is not to the point."

Carve a cherry pit with the utmost skill, and at best it is still a cherry pit; but a diamond, even if cut poorly, is still a precious stone. Even if a speaker cannot deliver an eloquent speech, if the subject is important, attempting to speak isn't useless. The subjects which we will cover at this time ought to be studied, and they are timely. I have chosen present and pressing truths, and if you will think them through for yourselves, the time you spend listening to this address will not be wasted.[1] I pray passionately that we may all benefit from this hour of reflection!

Happily, the topics are ones I can illustrate even while I am speaking to you. As a smith can teach his apprentice *while* making a horseshoe and *by* making a horseshoe, so we can make our own sermons examples of the doctrine they contain. In this case, we can practice while we preach, if the Lord is with us. A master chef instructs his pupils by following his own recipes. He prepares dishes in front of his audience, and while he describes the dishes and their preparation, he tastes the food himself, and his friends are refreshed as well. He will succeed by his delicious dishes, even if he is not a man of eloquent speech.

> If the topics we bring before our listeners are in themselves good, they will make up for our lack of skill in presenting them.

The person who serves food to others is surer of success than the one who only plays an instrument well – and leaves the audience with no memory but that of a pleasant sound. If the topics we bring before our listeners are in themselves good, they will make up for our lack of skill in presenting them. As long as the guests get the spiritual meat, the one who serves at the table may be happy to be forgotten.

Three Themes

My topics have to do with our lifework – with the

---

1   Remember, the contents of this book were first presented as a speech.

crusade against error and sin in which we are engaged. I hope every person here wears the red cross on his or her heart as a badge, and promises to act boldly for Christ and for His cross, and to never be satisfied until Christ's enemies are defeated and Christ Himself is satisfied. Our fathers used to speak of "the cause of God and truth," and it is for this that we bear arms, the few against the many, the feeble against the mighty. Oh, to be found good soldiers of Jesus Christ!

Three things are of the utmost importance just now, and indeed, they always have stood, and always will stand in the front rank for practical purposes. The first is *our armory* – our weapon, which is the inspired Word. The second is *our army*, the church of the living God, called out by Himself, which we must lead under our Lord's command. The third is *our strength*, by which we wear the armor and use the sword. The Holy Spirit is our power to be and to do, to suffer and to serve, to grow and to fight, to wrestle and to overcome. Our third theme is of main importance, and though we place it last, we rank it first.

Chapter 2

Our Armory

We will begin with our armory. That armory is to me, at any rate – and I hope it is to each one of you – the Bible. To us, Holy Scripture *is like the tower of David built for teaching, upon which there hang a thousand bucklers, all shields of mighty men* (Song of Solomon 4:4).

If we want weapons, we must come here for them, and here only. Whether we seek the sword of offense or the shield of defense, we must find it within the volume of inspiration – Scripture. If others have any other storehouse, I confess at once that I have none. I have nothing else to preach when I finish with the Bible. Indeed, I can have no wish to preach at all if I may not continue to expound the subjects which I find in these pages. What else is worth preaching? Brothers, the truth of God is the only treasure for which we seek, and Scripture is the only field in which we dig for it.

We don't need anything more than what God has

seen fit to reveal. Certain errant spirits are never at home until they are away. They crave for something which I think they will never find, either in heaven above, or in the earth beneath, or in the water under the earth, as long as they are in their present state of mind. They never rest, for they will have nothing to do with an infallible revelation, and so they are doomed to wander throughout time and eternity and find no permanent home.[2]

For the moment, they take pleasure as if they were satisfied with their latest new toy, but in a few months, it is amusing to them to break in pieces all the ideas which they formerly prepared with care and showed off with delight. They go up a hill only to come down again. Indeed, they say that the pursuit of truth is better than truth itself. They like fishing better than the fish, which may very well be true, since their fish are very small and very full of bones.

These men are as great at destroying their own theories as some paupers are at tearing up their clothes. They begin again numerous times; their house is always having its foundation excavated. They should be good at beginnings, for they have always been beginning since we have known them. They are as the rolling thing before the whirlwind, or they *are like the sea in tempest, that cannot rest, whose waters cast up mire and dirt* (Isaiah 57:20).

Although their cloud is not the cloud which represented the divine presence, yet it is always moving ahead of them, and their tents are scarcely pitched before

2   A reference to Hebrews 13:14, *continuing city* (JUB).

it is time for the stakes to be pulled up again. These men are not even seeking certainty; their heaven lies in shunning all fixed truth, and following every will-o'-the-wisp of speculation. They are ever learning, but they never come to the knowledge of the truth.

As for us, we cast an anchor in the haven of the Word of God. Here is our peace, our strength, our life, our motive, our hope, our happiness. God's Word is our ultimatum. Here we have it. Our understanding cries, "I have found it!" Our conscience proclaims that here is the truth, and here our heart finds a support to which all her affections can cling. So we rest content.

> God's Word is our ultimatum.

The Complete Word of God

If the revelation of God were not enough for our faith, what could we add to it? Who can answer this question? What would any person propose to add to the sacred Word? A moment's thought would lead us to search the most attractive words of men with the ridiculous idea that we could propose to add them to the Word of God.

It would be like piecing together fabric intended to be a solid piece. Would you add rags to a royal garment? Would you pile the filth of the streets in a king's treasury? Would you join the pebbles of the seashore to the diamonds of Golconda?[3]

For us to believe and to preach anything more than what the Word of God sets before us seems utterly

---

3   A region in India known for mines that have produced some of the world's most famous gems.

absurd to me. Yet we confront a generation of people who are always wanting to discover a new motivational power and a new gospel for their churches. The quilt covering their bed does not seem to be long enough, and they would gladly borrow a yard or two of wool from the Unitarian, the agnostic, or even the atheist.

If we find any spiritual force or heavenward power beyond what is reported in the Bible, I think we can do without it. Certainly, it must be such a sham that we are better without it. The Scriptures in their own sphere are like God in the universe – all-sufficient. All the light and power the mind of man can need in spiritual things is revealed in Scripture. *But all these things when they are reproved by the light are made manifest, for the light is that which manifests everything* (Ephesians 5:13).

False Motivation

We hear of other motivation beyond that which lies in the Scriptures, but we believe such a force to be exaggerated.

Imagine a train is derailed, or is otherwise unable to proceed, and a breakdown crew has arrived. They bring engines to move the big obstacle. At first, there seems to be no movement; the engine power is not enough.

But then someone speaks. A small boy has a solution.

He cries, "Father, if they don't have enough power, I will lend them my rocking horse to help them!"

We have had the offer of a considerable number of rocking horses of late. They have not accomplished much that I can see, but they promised a great deal. I fear their effect has been for evil rather than for good; they have moved the people to contempt, and have driven them out of the places of worship which they were once glad to fill.

The new toys have been exhibited, and the people, after seeing them for a little while, have moved on to other toy shops. These fine, new nothings have done no good, and they never will do any good while the world stands. The Word of God is quite sufficient to interest and bless the souls of men throughout all time, but novelties soon fail.

> My brothers, think by all means. But the thoughts of God are better than yours.

"Surely," someone cries, "we must add our own thoughts to that!"

My brothers, think by all means. But the thoughts of God are better than yours. You may shed fine thoughts, as trees in autumn cast their leaves, but there is One who knows more about your thoughts than you do, and He thinks little of them. Doesn't Scripture say, *The LORD knows the thoughts of man, that they are vanity* (Psalm 94:11)?

To liken *our* thoughts to the great thoughts of God would be a gross absurdity. Would you bring your candle to show the sun? Your nothingness to replenish the eternal all? It is better to be silent before the Lord than to dream of supplementing what He has spoken. The Word of the Lord is to the thoughts of men as a garden is to a wilderness.

Keep within the covers of the sacred Book, and you

are in the land which flows with milk and honey. Why seek to add to it the desert sands?

Keeping the Word Pure

Try not to discard anything from the perfect Book. If you find it there, there let it stand, and it is your responsibility to preach it in accordance with the alliance with, and the scope of, faith. Anything worthy of God's revealing is worthy of our preaching, and there is nothing we can take credit for in it.

> *Man does not live by bread alone, but by*
> *every word that proceeds out of the mouth of*
> *the LORD shall man live* (Deuteronomy 8:3).
> *Every word of God is pure: he is a shield*
> *unto those that put their trust in him*
> (Proverbs 30:5).

Let every revealed truth be presented when the time is right. Do not look somewhere else for a subject; with such limitless content before you, there is no need for you to search elsewhere. With such glorious truth to preach, it will be unrestrained wickedness if you do.

Testing Our Arsenal

We have already tested the competence of all this provision for our warfare; the weapons of our armory are the very best, for we have tried them and have found them to be so. Some of you younger brothers have only tested the Scriptures a little as of now. But others of us, who are now getting grey, can assure you that we have tried the Word and it has stood every test. We have found *The words of the LORD are pure words: as silver tried in a furnace of earth, purified seven times* (Psalm 12:6).

The sacred Word has endured more criticism than the best accepted form of philosophy or science, and it has survived every ordeal. As a living theologian has said, "After its present assailants are all dead, their funeral sermons will be preached from this Book – not one verse omitted – from the first page of Genesis to the last page of Revelation."

Some of us have lived for many years, in daily conflict, perpetually putting the Word of God to the test, and we can honestly give you this assurance: it is sufficient for every crisis. After using this double-edged sword upon coats of mail and brass shields, we find no nick or gouge in its edge. It is neither broken nor dulled in the fight. It would split the devil himself in half, from the crown of his head to the sole of his foot, and yet it would show no sign of failure whatsoever.

> The sacred Word has endured more criticism than the best accepted form of philosophy or science, and it has survived every ordeal.

Today, it is still the identical mighty Word of God that it was in the hands of our Lord Jesus. How it strengthens us when we remember the many conquests of souls which we have achieved through the sword of the Spirit!

Have any of you heard of a conversion brought about by any other doctrine than that which is in the Word? I would like to have a book that lists conversions produced by modern theology. I would order a copy of such a publication. I will not say what I might do with it after I had read it, but I would at least increase its sale by one copy just to see what progressive theology pretends to have done.

What examples might that list contain? Conversions through the doctrines of universal reconciliation.[4] Conversions through doubtful doctrine. Conversions to the love of God and to faith in Jesus Christ, but by hearing that the death of the Savior was only the consummation of a grand example, but not a substitutionary sacrifice. Conversions by a gospel out of which all the gospel has been drained.

They say wonders will never cease, but such wonders will never begin. Let them report changes of heart brought about in these ways, and give us an opportunity to test them. Then, perhaps, we may consider whether it is worth our while to walk away from that Word – which we have tried in hundreds and, some of us here, in many thousands of situations, and have always found it effective for salvation.

We know why they sneer at conversions. These are grapes which such foxes cannot reach, and therefore, rather than admit defeat, they will declare they must be sour.[5] As we believe in the new birth, and expect to see it in thousands of cases, we will hold to that Word of Truth by which the Holy Spirit works regeneration. In a word, in our warfare we will continue using the

---

4   The unbiblical belief that every human being will at some point, either now or after they die, be reconciled with God so that none will go to hell.

5   Reference to the fable of the Fox and the Grapes.

old weapon of the sword of the Spirit, until we can find something better. At present, our verdict is: *There is none like that; give it to me.*[6]

The Word as Comfort

How often we have seen how the Word is effective for comfort! It is, as one brother expressed it in prayer, a difficult thing to deal with broken hearts. I have felt like such a fool when trying to help deliver a prisoner from Giant Despair's castle![7] It is so difficult to help someone change from despondency to hope. I have tried to trap my game, so to speak, by every method I know, but when almost in my grasp, the creature has burrowed another hole! I had dug him out of twenty already, and then have had to begin again.

> Within the Scriptures there is a balm for every wound, a salve for every sore.

The convicted sinner uses all kinds of arguments to prove he cannot be saved. The inventions of despair are as many as the devices of self-confidence. There is no letting light into the dark cellar of doubt, except through the window of the Word of God. Within the Scriptures there is a balm for every wound, a salve for every sore. Oh, the wondrous power in the Scriptures to create a soul of hope within the ribs of despair, and bring eternal light into the darkness, which has made a long midnight in the inmost soul!

Often have we tried the Word of the Lord as "the

6   Spoken by King David of Goliath's sword in 1 Samuel 21:9.

7   A reference from *The Pilgrim's Progress.*

cup of consolation," and it has never failed to cheer those who despair. We know what we say, because we have witnessed the blessed facts: the Scriptures of truth, applied by the Holy Spirit, have brought peace and joy to those who sat in darkness and in the valley of the shadow of death.

The Power of Scripture

We have also observed the excellence of the Word in the edification of believers, and in the production of righteousness, holiness, and usefulness. We are always being told, in these days, of the "ethical" side of the gospel. I pity those to whom this is a novelty. Haven't they discovered this before? We have always been dealing with the ethical side of the gospel; indeed, we find it ethical all over. There is no true doctrine which has not been fruitful in good works. Payson[8] wisely said, "If there is one fact, one doctrine, or promise in the Bible, which has produced no practical effect upon your temper or conduct, be assured that you do not truly believe it."

All scriptural teaching has its practical purpose and its practical result. And what we have to say, not as a matter of discovery, but as a matter of plain common sense, is this: if we have had fewer fruits than we would desire to have *with* the tree, we suspect there will be no fruit at all when the tree has gone, and the roots are dug up.

The very root of holiness lies in the gospel of our Lord Jesus Christ, and if we remove this and take a

---

8   Edward Payson (1783-1827).

view grounded in more fruitfulness, we make the most astounding mistake. We have seen a fine morality, a stern integrity, a delicate purity, and, what is more, a devout holiness, produced by the doctrines of grace. We see people living in devotion to Christ; we see calm acceptance when suffering comes; we see joyful confidence at the moment of death; and we see these not in a few instances, but as the general outcome of intelligent faith in the teachings of Scripture.

We have even wondered at the sacred result of the old gospel. Though we are often accustomed to seeing it, it never loses its charm. We have seen poor men and women yielding themselves to Christ, and living for Him in a way that has made our hearts bow in adoration of the God of grace. We have said, "This must be a true gospel which can produce such lives as these."

The very root of holiness lies in the gospel of our Lord Jesus Christ.

If we have not talked so much about ethics as some have done, we remember an old saying of the country folk: "Go to such a place to *hear* about good works, but go to another place to *see* them." Much talk, little work. Great cry is the token of little wool – a lot of fuss over nothing.[9] Some have preached good works until there is barely a decent person left in the congregation, while others have preached free grace and dying love in such a way that sinners have become saints, and saints have been as boughs loaded down with fruit to the praise

---

9 An expression meaning a great deal of fuss and protesting over something of little or no substance or importance.

and glory of God. Having seen the harvest which comes from what we have planted, we are not going to change it at the commands of this whimsical age.

We have especially seen and tested the effectiveness of the Word of God when we have been by someone's sickbed. A few days ago, I was by the side of one of our elders, who appeared to be dying, and it was like heaven on earth to talk with him. I never saw so much joy at a wedding as I saw in that quiet room. He hoped to be with Jesus soon, and he was joyful in the prospect.

He said, "I have no doubt, no cloud, no trouble, no want. I do not even have a wish. The doctrine you have taught has served me to live by, and now it serves me to die by. I am resting upon the precious blood of Christ, and it is a firm foundation." And he added, "How silly all those letters against the gospel now appear to me! I have read some of them, and I have noted the attacks upon the old faith, but they seem quite absurd to me now that I lie on the verge of eternity. What could the new doctrine do for me now?"

I came away from my conversation greatly strengthened and gladdened by the good man's testimony, and all the more, I was personally comforted because it was the Word which I myself had constantly preached that had been such a blessing to my friend. If God had used the message from such a poor instrument, I felt the Word itself must be good for sure. I am never as happy amid all the shouts of youthful celebration as I am on a day when I hear the dying testimony of one who is resting on the everlasting gospel of the grace of God. The ultimate issue, as seen upon a deathbed, is a true test, as it is an inevitable one. Preach that which will enable men to face death without fear, and you will preach nothing but the old gospel.

Brothers, we will clothe ourselves in that which God has supplied us with in the armory of inspired Scripture, because every weapon in it has been tried and proved in many ways, and never has any part of our suit of armor failed us.

Moreover, we will always keep to the Word of God, because we have had experience of its power within ourselves. It is not so long ago that you will have forgotten how, like a hammer, the Word of God broke your stony heart, and brought down your stubborn will. By the Word of the Lord you were brought to the cross and comforted by the reconciliation Christ offers, and whose sacrifice pays sin's penalty and restores our relationship with God. That Word breathed a new life into you, and when, for the first time, you knew you were a child of God, you felt the uplifting power of the gospel received by faith. The Holy Spirit brought about your salvation through the Holy Scriptures. You trace your conversion, I am sure, to the Word of the Lord; for this alone is *perfect, converting the soul* (Psalm 19:7).

Whoever may have been the person who said it, or whatever may have been the book in which you read it, it was not man's word, nor man's thoughts upon God's Word, but the Word itself, which made you

> Preach that which will enable men to face death without fear, and you will preach nothing but the old gospel.

know salvation in the Lord Jesus. It was neither human reasoning, nor the power of eloquent speech, nor the power of moral persuasion, but the omnipotence – the all-powerful authority – of the Spirit, applying the Word itself, that gave you rest and peace and joy through believing. We are ourselves trophies of the power of the sword of the Spirit; He leads us in triumph in every place, the willing captives of His grace. No one should be surprised that we stay close to it.

How many times since conversion has Holy Scripture been everything to you? You have your weak moments, I suppose. But haven't you been restored by the precious medicine of the promise of the Faithful One? A passage of Scripture applied speedily to the heart accelerates the weak heart into mighty action. Men speak of waters that revive the spirits, and tonics that strengthen a person's state of health and mind, but the Word of God has been more than this to us more times than we can count.

Amid sharp and strong temptations, and fierce and bitter trials, the Word of the Lord has preserved us. Amid discouragements which restrained our hopes, and disappointments which wounded our hearts, we have felt ourselves strong to act and endure, because the assurances of help which we find in our Bibles have brought us a secret, unconquerable energy.

The Word Uplifts

Brothers, we have experienced the boost which the Word of God can give us – the uplifting toward God and heaven. If you begin studying books contrary to the inspired Word of God, aren't you aware of slipping downward? I have known some to whom such reading has been like a noxious stench surrounding them with the cold, clammy sweat of death. Yes, and I may add, that to forego your Bible reading for the reading of even good books would soon bring a conscious sinking of the soul.

Haven't you found that even decent books may be to you like a flat land to look down upon, rather than as a summit to which you could aspire? You have come up to their level long ago, and get no higher by reading them. It is pointless to spend precious time on them.

Was it ever this way with you and the Bible? Did you ever rise above its simplest teaching, and feel that it tended to draw you downward? Never! In proportion as your mind becomes saturated with Holy Scripture, you are conscious of being lifted right up and carried upward as if on eagles' wings. You seldom come down from a solitary Bible reading without feeling you have drawn near to God. I say a solitary one, for when reading with others, the danger is that uninspired comments may be flies in the pot of ointment – one can spoil the whole batch.[10] The prayerful study of the Word is not only a means of instruction, but also an act of devotion in which the transforming power of grace is often exercised, and which changes us into the image of the One whom the Word mirrors to us. Is there anything, after all, like the Word of God when the open Book finds open hearts?

10 An expression based on Ecclesiastes 10:1: *Dead flies cause the oint-ment of the apothecary to send forth a stinking savour: likewise a small act of folly unto him that is esteemed for wisdom and honour.*

When I read the lives of such men as Richard Baxter,[11] David Brainerd,[12] Robert Murray McCheyne,[13] and many others, why, I feel like one who has bathed himself in some cool brook after having journeyed through a dark country, which left him dusty and depressed. I feel this way because such men embodied Scripture in their lives and illustrated it in their experience. They had the washing of water by the Word, and this is what we need. We must get it where they found it. To see the effects of the truth of God in the lives of holy men confirms faith and encourages holy aspiration.

A Word of Caution

Other influences do not help us toward this type of supreme ideal of holiness – being set apart for Christ. If you read what we might think of as the Babylonian books of the present day, you will catch their spirit – and it is a foreign one – which will draw you aside from the Lord your God. You may also experience great harm from theologians who pretend to speak the Jerusalem dialect – the language of God's people, but their speech is half of Ashdod[14] – the language of foreigners who aren't followers of God. These will confuse your mind and corrupt your faith. It is possible that a book which is excellent for the most part, but

---

11   English Puritan church leader, poet, hymnwriter, and theologian Richard Baxter (1615-1691).

12   American missionary David Brainerd (1718-1747).

13   Scottish preacher Robert Murray McCheyne (1813-1843), also spelled M'Cheyne.

14   A Philistine city. The term is taken from Nehemiah 13:23-24. See also Isaiah 20:1.

which has a little tainted content, may do you more harm than a thoroughly bad book.

Be careful, for books of this kind come forth from the press like clouds of locusts. Galatians 5:9 warns about false teaching, comparing it to how yeast works, when it says *a little leaven leavens the whole lump*. In these days, you can scarcely find a book that is free from the modern leaven, and the least particle of it ferments until it produces the wildest inaccuracy. In reading books of the new order, though no palpable falsehood may appear, you are conscious of a twist being given to you, and a sense of

> With your Bible you may always feel at ease; there every breath from every part of it brings life and health.

sinking in your spirit. Therefore, be on your guard. But with your Bible you may always feel at ease; there every breath from every part of it brings life and health. If you stay close to the inspired Book, you can suffer no harm. In other words, you are at the source of all moral and spiritual good. This is proper food for people of God; this is the bread which nourishes the highest life.

An Endless Source for Study

After preaching the gospel for forty years, and after printing the sermons I have preached for more than thirty-six years, reaching now to the number of twenty-two hundred in weekly succession, I am fairly entitled to speak about the fullness and richness of the Bible as a preacher's book. Brothers, it is inexhaustible. No question about freshness will arise if we stay close to the text of the sacred book. It shouldn't be difficult to find topics totally distinct from those we have taught on before; the variety is as infinite as the fullness. A long life will only be enough for us to go around the shores of this great continent of light.

In the forty years of my own ministry, I have only touched the hem of the garment of divine truth, but what virtue has flowed out of it! The Word is like its author: infinite, immeasurable, without end. If you were ordained to be a preacher throughout eternity, you would have enough material in your hands to equal everlasting demands.

Brothers, shall we each have a pulpit somewhere among the planets? Shall we have a church of millions of people? Shall we have voices strong enough to reach attentive constellations? Shall we be witnesses for the Lord of grace to myriads of worlds which will be struck with wonder when they hear of the incarnate God? Shall we be surrounded by pure minds inquiring and searching into the mystery of God appearing in the flesh? Will the unfallen worlds desire to be instructed in the glorious gospel of the blessed God? Will each one of us have our own tale to tell of our experience of infinite love? I think so, since the Lord has saved us *To the intent that now unto the principalities and powers in heavenly places might be known by the congregation the manifold wisdom of God* (Ephesians 3:10). If this is how it will be, our Bibles will suffice for ages to come for new topics every morning, and for fresh songs and sermons forever.

Knowing the Word

We are determined, then, since we have this arsenal supplied for us by the Lord, and since we want no other, to use the Word of God only, and to use it with greater energy. We are resolved – and I hope there is no opposition among us – to know our Bibles better. Do we know the sacred volume half as well as we should know it? Have we worked to gain as much knowledge of the Word of God as many experts have obtained about a favorite classic? Isn't it possible we still discover passages of Scripture which are new to us? Should it be so? Is there any part of what the Lord has written that you have never read?

I was struck with my brother Archibald Brown's[15] observation who thought that unless he read the Scriptures through from end to end, there might be inspired teachings which he might never know. So, he resolved to read the books in order, and, having done so once, he continued the habit. Have any of us failed to do this? Let's begin at once.

I love to see how readily certain ones of our associates find an appropriate passage, and then quote its parallel, and crown all with a third. They seem to know exactly the passage which strikes the nail on the head. They have their Bibles, not only in their hearts, but also at their finger tips. This is a most valuable achievement for a minister. An expert Bible scholar is a good theologian.

---

15   Archibald Geikie Brown (1844-1922). A student, friend, and associate of Charles Spurgeon. He became Spurgeon's successor.

Handling Scripture Accurately

Certain others, whom I appreciate for other things, are still weak on this point, and seldom quote a passage of Scripture correctly. Certainly, their alterations have an unpleasant effect on the ear of the Bible reader. It is sadly common among ministers to add a word or subtract a word from the passage, or in some way to dishonor the language of Scripture.

How often have I heard comrades speak about making "your calling and salvation" sure! Possibly, they didn't enjoy the Calvinistic word *election* as much as we do, and therefore they allowed it to disappear. Others quote half a text and miss the meaning – actually, in some cases they contradict it. Our reverence for the great author of Scripture should prevent all tampering with His words. No alteration of Scripture can by any possibility be an improvement. Believers in verbal inspiration should be studiously careful to be verbally correct.

Those who believe they see errors in Scripture may think they are competent to modify the language of the Lord of Hosts, but those of us who believe God and accept the very words He uses, may not make such an overconfident attempt. Let's quote the words as they are in the best possible translation, and it is even better if we know the original, and can tell if our version fails to give a sense of the true meaning. How much trouble may arise out of an accidental alteration of the Word! Blessed are those who are in accord with the divine teaching and receive its true meaning as the Holy Spirit teaches them! Oh, that we might know the

Spirit of Holy Scripture thoroughly, drinking it in, until we are saturated with it! This is the blessing which we resolve to obtain.

Believing Scripture

By God's grace we intend to believe the Word of God more intensely. There is believing, and there is believing. You believe in all your associates who are gathered here, but in some of them you have a conscious practical confidence, since in your hour of trouble they have come to your rescue and proved themselves brothers born for adversity. You confide in these with absolute certainty, because you have personally tested them. Your faith was faith before, but now it is a higher, firmer, and more assured confidence.

> Oh, that we might know the Spirit of Holy Scripture thoroughly, drinking it in, until we are saturated with it!

Believe in the inspired Scripture completely. Believe it right through. Believe it thoroughly. Believe it with the whole strength of your being. Let the truths of Scripture become the chief factors in your life, the chief operative forces of your action. Let the great concepts of the gospel story be to you as certain, essential facts as any fact which you come across in everyday life at home or in the outside world. Let them be as vividly true to you as your own ever-present body, with its aches and pains, its appetites and joys. If we can get out of the realm of fiction and fancy, and into the world of fact, we will have struck a vein of power which will yield us an immeasurable treasure of strength. Thus, to become mighty in the Scriptures will be to become mighty through God.

We should also resolve that we will quote more of Holy Scripture. Sermons should be full of the Bible, sweetened, strengthened, and sanctified with Bible essence. Outgrowths of Scripture are the kinds of sermons people need to hear. If they do not love to hear them, this is all the more reason why we should preach Scripture to them. The gospel has the singular ability to create a taste for itself. Bible hearers, when they hear indeed, come to be Bible lovers. The mere stringing of texts together is a poor way of making sermons, though some have tried it, and I don't doubt God has blessed them, since they did their best. It is far better to string texts together than to pour out one's own poor thoughts in a watered-down flood. There will at least be something to be thought of and remembered if we quote the Holy Word. With our own thoughts, there may be nothing to be thought of and remembered.

Texts of Scripture do not need to be strung together; they may be appropriately included to give sharpness and a point to a sermon. They will be the power of the sermon. Our own words are mere paper pellets compared with the rifle shot of the Word. Scripture is the conclusion of the whole matter. There is no arguing after we discover *It is written*. To a large extent, in the hearts and consciences of our hearers, the debate is over when the Lord has spoken. *Thus saith the LORD* is the end of discussion to Christian minds, and even the ungodly cannot resist Scripture without resisting the Spirit who wrote it. We will speak scripturally if we are to convince our hearers.

The Word of God Only

We are further resolved that we will preach nothing but the Word of God. What separates the crowd from hearing the gospel is largely the sad fact that it is not always the gospel they hear if they go to places of worship. All else falls short of what their souls need.

Have you heard of the king who made a series of great feasts and invited many people week after week? He had a number of servants whom he appointed to wait at his table, and these served on the assigned days and spoke with the people. But somehow, after a while, the bulk of the people did not come to the feasts. Fewer and fewer came, and most of the citizens turned their backs on the banquets.

The king asked around, and he discovered that the food he provided did not seem to satisfy those who attended the banquets, and so they stopped coming. He decided he would examine the tables and the meats served on them. He realized he had plentiful provisions and many serving pieces that never came out of his storehouses.

He looked at the food and he said, "But how is this? How did these entrées come to be here? I did not provide these. My oxen and my young animals were killed, yet here we do not have the meat of fattened cattle, but hard meat from lean and starved cattle. There are bones here, but where is the fat and the marrow? The bread also is coarse, whereas mine was made of the finest of wheat. The wine is mixed with water, and the water is not from a pure well."

One of those who stood by answered and said, "O king, we thought the people would overindulge with marrow and fatness, and so we gave them bone and gristle. We thought also they would be weary of the best white bread, and so we baked a little at our own homes – bread in which the bran and husks were allowed to remain. It is the opinion of the educated that our provision is more suitable for these times than that which your majesty prescribed so long ago. As for the sediment in the wines, the tastes of people these days have changed, and pure water is so transparent that it is too light of a drink for men who are accustomed to drinking from the river of Egypt, which has a taste in it of mud from the Mountains of the Moon."

Then the king knew why the people didn't come to the feast.

Is this similar to the reason for why going to the house of God has become so distasteful to so many of the population? I believe it is. Have our Lord's servants been chopping up their own odds and ends and tainted bits to make a cheap minced meat product[16] with them for the millions, and do the millions therefore turn away? Listen to the rest of my parable.

"Clear the tables!" cried the king in indignation. "Cast that rubbish to the dogs. Bring in the beef roasts and set forth my royal food. Remove those worthless

---

16   The term "potted meat" that Spurgeon originally used here is similar
      to what we would see in Spam or bologna.

things from the hall, and that contaminated bread from the table, and get rid of the water of the muddy river."

They did so, and if my parable is right, very soon there was a rumor throughout the streets that truly royal delicacies were to be served. The people flocked to the palace, and the king's name became exceedingly great throughout the land.

Let's try the plan. Maybe we will soon rejoice to see our Master's banquet filled with guests.

We are resolved, then, to use more fully than ever what God has provided for us in this Book, for we are sure of its inspiration.[17] Let me say that over again. We are sure of its inspiration. You will notice there are those who will frequently attack as if going against verbal inspiration of Scripture. The form chosen is a mere ploy. Verbal inspiration is the presumed target of the assault, but the

> Have our Lord's servants been chopping up their own odds and ends and tainted bits to make a cheap minced meat product?

attack is really aimed at inspiration itself. You will not read far in one of their essays before you will find that the gentleman who started by contesting a theory of inspiration which none of us ever held, will wind up by showing his hand, and that hand wages war with inspiration itself.

There is the true point. We don't care much for any theory of inspiration; in fact, we have none. To us, the complete verbal inspiration of Holy Scripture is fact and

---

17   Meaning, we're confident the authors of the Bible wrote under the divine inspiration of the Holy Spirit.

not hypothesis. It is a shame to theorize about a deeply mysterious subject that makes an argument based on faith rather than on fancy. Believe in the inspiration of Scripture, and believe it in the most intense sense. You will not believe in a truer and fuller inspiration than really exists. No one is likely to err in that direction, even if error is possible. If you adopt theories which strip off a portion here, and deny authority to a passage there, you will eventually have no inspiration left that is worthy of the name.

The Infallible Word

If this Book is not infallible, where will we find infallibility? We have abandoned the pope,[18] for he has blundered often and terribly, but we will not replace him with a horde of little popes fresh from college. Are these correctors of Scripture – textual experts – infallible that we would follow them? Is it certain that our Bibles are not right, but that the experts must be right?

The old silver is to be depreciated, but the German silver, which is put in its place, is to be assigned the value of gold. Young people who have just finished reading the latest novel correct the ideas of their fathers, who were men of weight and character. Doctrines which produced the godliest generation that ever lived on the face of the earth are scrutinized as sheer foolishness. Nothing is as obnoxious to these persons as that which has the smell of Puritanism. Young people turn up their noses at the very sound of the word *Puritan*.

---

18   In 1891, at the time of Spurgeon's speech, the pope was Pope Leo XIII, who served from 1878 to 1903.

Though if the Puritans were here again, they would not dare to treat them so dismissively, for if Puritans did fight, they were soon known as Ironsides, and their leader could hardly be called a fool, even by those who stigmatized him as a tyrant.

Surely, we wouldn't say Oliver Cromwell[19] and the men who were with him were all weak-minded persons, would we? It is strange that these are praised to the heavens by the very men who ridicule their true successors, believers in the same faith. But where shall infallibility be found? *The deep saith, It is not in me* (Job 28:14), yet those who have no depth at all would have us imagine that it is in them, or else by perpetual change they hope to land on it.

Are we to believe infallibility is with educated men?

Are we to believe infallibility is with educated men? We might find it absurd to say, "Now, Farmer Smith, when you have read your Bible, and have enjoyed its precious promises, tomorrow morning you will have to go down the street to ask the scholarly man at the parsonage whether this portion of Scripture belongs to the inspired part of the Word, or whether it is of unsure authority. It will be well for you to know whether it was written by *the* Isaiah, or whether it was by the second of the two Obadiahs."

In this case, all possibility of certainty is transferred from the spiritual man to a class of persons whose scholarship is showy, but who do not even pretend to

---

19   Oliver Cromwell (1599-1658), an outspoken Puritan. He was an English military and political leader, and served as Lord Protector of the Commonwealth of England, Scotland, and Ireland.

have spirituality. We will gradually become so insecure and criticized, that only a few of the most profound will know what is in the Bible and what is not, and they will dictate to the rest of us. I have no more faith in their mercy than in their accuracy; they will rob us of all that we hold most dear and will take pleasure in the cruel achievement.

We will not endure this same reign of terror, for we still believe God reveals Himself more to spiritual infants than to the wise and shrewd, and we are sure that our own old English version of the Scriptures is sufficient for plain men for all purposes of life, salvation, and godliness. We do not despise learning, but we will never say of culture or criticism, *These are thy gods, O Israel* (Exodus 32:4, 8).

Do you see why men would lower the degree of inspiration in Scripture and would gladly reduce it to a microscopic quantity? It is because the truth of God is to be replaced. Imagine if you go into a store in the evening to buy certain items which have a quality of color and texture that should be examined by daylight, or the best light possible. If, after you have entered the store, the salesman lowers the lights, or turns off the lights, and then begins to show you his merchandise, wouldn't your suspicions be aroused? Wouldn't you conclude that he is trying to pass off an inferior item to you? I more than suspect this is the little game of the inspiration depreciators.

Whenever a man begins to lower your view of inspiration, it is because he has a trick to play, which is not easily performed in the light. He would hold a figurative séance of evil spirits, and therefore he cries, "Turn down the lights!" We, brothers, are willing to ascribe to the Word of God all the inspiration that can possibly be ascribed to it, and we say boldly that if our preaching is not according to this Word, it is because there is no light in it. We are willing to be tried and tested by it in every way, and we consider the greatest of our hearers to be those who search the Scriptures daily to see whether these things are true. But to those who belittle inspiration, we will not subject ourselves to even an hour of their influence.

Science, Philosophy, and Religion

Do I hear someone say, "But still you must submit to the conclusions of science"? No one is more ready than we are to accept the evident facts of science. But what do you mean by science? Is the thing called science infallible? Isn't science falsely called this? The history of that human ignorance which calls itself philosophy is absolutely identical to the history of fools, except where it separates into foolishness.

If another Erasmus[20] were to arise and write the history of foolishness, he would have to give several chapters to philosophy and science, and those chapters would be more telling than any others. I myself would not dare to say that philosophers and scientists are generally fools, but I would give them liberty to speak about one another, and at the close I would say,

---

20   Desiderius Erasmus Roterodamus (1466-1536), a Dutch Renaissance humanist, Catholic priest, social critic, teacher, and theologian.

"Gentlemen, you are less complimentary to each other than I would have been."

I would let the wise of each generation speak of the generation that went before it, or nowadays each half of a generation might deal with the previous half-generation, for there is little of theory in science today which will survive twenty years, and only a little more which will see the first day of the twentieth century.

We travel now at such a rapid rate that we rush by sets of scientific hypotheses as quickly as we pass telegraph posts when riding in an express train. All that we are certain of today is this: what the scholars were sure of a few years ago is now thrown into the limbo of discarded errors. I believe in science, but not in what is called *science*. No proven fact in nature is opposed to revelation.

We cannot reconcile the pretty speculations of those who make grandiose claims with the truths of the Bible, and we would not even if we could. I feel like the man who said, "I can understand to some degree how these great men have found out the weight of the stars and their distances from one another, and even how, by the spectroscope, they have discovered the materials of which they are composed. But I cannot guess how they found out their names." I agree.

The fanciful part of science, which is prized by so many, is what we do not accept. That is the important part of science to many – that part which is a mere guess – for which the guessers fight tooth and nail. The mythology of science is as false as the mythology of the heathen, but this is the thing which some make into a god. I say again, as far as its facts are concerned, that science is never in conflict with the truths of Holy Scripture, but the hurried deductions drawn from those facts, and the inventions classified as facts, are opposed to Scripture, and necessarily so, because falsehood does not agree with truth.

Two sorts of people have produced great mischief, and yet neither of them is worth being considered as a judge in the matter; they are both disqualified. It is essential that an umpire know both sides of a question, and neither of these has enough information to discern anything.

We cannot reconcile the pretty speculations of those who make grandiose claims with the truths of the Bible, and we would not even if we could.

The first is the nonreligious scientist. What does he know about religion? What can he know? He is out of court when the question is, does science agree with religion? Obviously, the one who would answer this question must know both of the two things in the question.

The second is a better man, but capable of even more trouble. I mean the unscientific Christian, who will trouble his head about reconciling the Bible with science. He had better leave it alone and not begin tampering with it. The mistake made by such men has been that in trying to solve a difficulty, they have either twisted the Bible or contorted science. The solution has soon been seen to be erroneous, and then we hear the cry that Scripture has been defeated. Not at all, not at all. It is only a worldly luster on it that has been removed.

Here is an example of a good brother who writes a wonderful book to prove that the six days of creation represent six great geological periods, and he shows how the geological strata, and the organisms in it, follow very much in the order of the Genesis story of creation. It may be so, or it may not be so, but if before long anybody would show that the strata do not lie in any such order, what would my reply be?

I would say that the Bible never taught that they did. The Bible said, *In the beginning God created the heavens and the earth* (Genesis 1:1). That leaves any length of time for your fire ages and your ice ages and all that, before the creation of the present age of man. Then we reach the six days in which the Lord made the heavens and the earth, and rested on the seventh day. There is nothing said about long ages of time, but, on the contrary, it says in Genesis 1: *And the evening and the morning were the first day*, and *the evening and the morning were the second* day, and so on. I am not laying down any theory here, but simply saying that if our friend's great book is all nonsense, the Bible is not responsible for it. It is true that his theory has an appearance of support from the parallelism which he makes out between the organic life of the ages and that of the seven days, but this may be accounted for by the fact that God usually follows a certain order, whether He works in long periods or in short ones. I do not know, and I do not care much about the question, but I want to say that if you smash up an explanation, you must not imagine that you have damaged the scriptural truth which seemed to require the explanation.

You have only burned the wooden palisades (walls made of wooden posts) with which well-meaning men thought to protect an impenetrable fort which needed no such defense.

For the most part, we had better leave a difficulty where it is, rather than make another difficulty by our theory. Why make a second hole in the kettle to mend the first? Especially when the first hole is not there at all, and needs no mending. Believe everything in science which is proved; it will not come to much. You do not need to fear that your faith will be overburdened. And then believe everything which is clearly in the Word of God, whether it is proved by outside evidence or not. No proof is needed when God speaks. If He has said it, this is evidence enough.

> No proof is needed when God speaks. If He has said it, this is evidence enough.

But we are told that we ought to give up a part of our old-fashioned theology to save the rest. We are in a carriage travelling over the steppes (grassland plains) of Russia. The coachman is driving the horses furiously, but the wolves are close upon us! There they are! Can't you see their eyes of fire? The danger is pressing. What must we do?

It is proposed that we throw out a child or two. By the time they have eaten the baby, we will have made a little headway, but if they overtake us again, what then? Why, brave man, throw out your wife! A man will give up all that he has for his life; he will give up nearly every truth in the hope of saving one.

Throw out inspiration, and let the critics devour it. Throw out election, and all the old Calvinism; this will be a delicious feast for the wolves, and the gentlemen who give us the sage advice will be glad to see the doctrines of grace torn limb from limb. Throw out natural depravity, eternal punishment, and the effectiveness of prayer. We have lightened the carriage wonderfully.

Now for another drop. Sacrifice the great sacrifice. Be done with the atonement! Brothers, this advice is villainous and murderous. We will escape these wolves with everything, or we will be lost with everything. It will be the truth, the whole truth, and nothing but the truth, or none at all. We will never attempt to save half the truth by casting any part of it away. The wise advice which has been given to us involves treason to God and disappointment to ourselves. We will stand by all or none. We will have a whole Bible or no Bible.

We are told that if we give up something, the adversaries will also give up something; but we don't care what they will do, for we are not afraid of them in the least. They are not the imperial conquerors they think themselves to be. We ask for no part of their insignificance. We are of the mind of the warrior who was offered presents to buy him off, and he was told that if he accepted so much gold or territory then he could return home in triumph, and glory in his easy gain. But he said, "The Greeks set no store by concessions. They find their glory not in presents, but in spoils."

With the sword of the Spirit we will maintain the whole truth as ours, and will not accept a part of it as a grant from the enemies of God. The truth of God we will maintain as the truth of God, and we will not retain it because the philosophic mind consents to our doing so. If scientists agree to our believing a part of the Bible, we thank them for nothing; we believe it whether or not they agree. Their agreement is of no more consequence to our faith than the consent of a Frenchman to the Englishman's holding London, or the consent of the mole to the eagle's sight. With God with us, we will not cease from this rejoicing, but will hold the whole of revealed truth, even to the end.

But now, brothers, while discussing this first part of my topic, perhaps at too great a length, I say to you that, believing this, we accept the obligation to preach everything which we see to be in the Word of God, as far as we see

> **We will never attempt to save half the truth by casting any part of it away.**

it. We would not willfully leave out any portion of the whole revelation of God, but we long to be able to say at the last, "We have not shunned to declare unto you the whole counsel of God." What trouble may come if we leave out any portion of the truth, or put in an alien element!

All good men will not agree with me when I say that the addition of infant baptism to the Word of God – for it certainly is not there – is fraught with trouble. Baptismal regeneration rides in upon the shoulders of pedobaptism – infant baptism.

But I speak now what I know. I have received letters from missionaries, not Baptists, but Wesleyans and Congregationalists, who have said to me, "Since we have been here [I will not mention the localities lest I get the good men into trouble], we find a class of persons who are the children of former converts, and who have been baptized, and are therefore called Christians, but they are not one whit better than the heathen around them. They seem to think that they are Christians because of their baptism, and, at the same time, the heathen think they are Christians, and their evil lives are a perpetual scandal and a dreadful stumbling block."

In many cases, this is true. I only use the fact as an illustration. But suppose it is either some other error invented, or some great truth neglected – evil will come of it. In the case of the terrible truths known by us as "the terrors of the Lord," their omission is producing the saddest results.

Omit Nothing from Truth

A good man who does not exactly teach the truth on this serious subject has, nevertheless, most faithfully written again and again to the papers to say that the great weakness of the modern pulpit is that it ignores the justice of God and the punishment of sin. His witness is true, and the evil which he indicates is immensely great. You cannot leave out those parts of the truth, which are so dark and so solemn, without weakening the force of all the other truths you preach. If you leave them out, you rob the truths which concern salvation from the wrath to come of their brightness and their urgent importance.

Comrades, leave out nothing. Be bold enough to

preach unpalatable and unpopular truth. The evil which we may do by adding to or taking from the Word of the Lord may not happen in our own days, but if it should come to maturity in another generation, we will be equally guilty. I have no doubt that the omission of certain truths by the earlier churches later led to serious error, while certain additions in the form of rites and ceremonies, which appeared innocent enough in themselves, led up to ritualism, and afterwards to the great apostasy of Romanism.

> You cannot leave out those parts of the truth, which are so dark and so solemn, without weakening the force of all the other truths you preach.

Be very careful. Do not go an inch beyond the line of Scripture, and do not stay an inch on this side of it. Stay on the straight line of the Word of God, as far as the Holy Spirit has taught you, and hold back nothing which He has revealed.

Do not be so bold as to abolish the two ordinances which the Lord Jesus has ordained, though some have ventured to abolish them. Neither should you exaggerate those ordinances into preordained channels of grace, as others have illogically done. Stay true to the revelation of the Spirit. Remember, you will have to give an account, and that account will not be with joy if you have played falsely with God's truth.

Remember the story of Gylippus, the Spartan general of the fifth century BC, to whom Lysander entrusted bags of gold to take to the city authorities. Those bags were tied at the mouth, and then sealed, and Gylippus thought that if he cut the bags at the bottom he might remove some of the coins, and then he could carefully sew the bottom up again, and so the seals would not be broken, and no one would suspect that gold had been taken. To his horror and surprise, when the bags were opened, there was a note in each bag stating how much it should contain, and so he was found out.

The Word of God has self-verifying clauses in it, so that you cannot run away with a part of it without the remainder of it accusing and convicting you. How will you answer for it at the judgement day if you have added to, or taken from, the Word of the Lord? I am not here to decide what you ought to consider to be the truth of God, and if I differ from you, or you from me, we shall not differ very much, if we are equally honest, straightforward, and God-fearing. The way to peace is not in disguising convictions, but in the honest expression of them in the power of the Holy Spirit.

One more word. We accept the obligation to preach all that is in God's Word definitely and distinctly. Don't many preach an open-ended truth indefinitely, and handle the Word of God deceitfully? You might join their ministry for years and not know what they believe. I heard about a certain cautious minister who was asked by a hearer, "What is your view of the atonement?"

He answered, "My dear sir, that is just what I have never told anybody, and *you* are not going to get it out of me."

This is a strange moral condition for the mind of a preacher of the gospel. I fear that he is not alone in this hesitancy to answer. They say, "They consume their own smoke"; that is to say, they keep their doubts for home consumption.

Many dare not say in the pulpit what they will say behind closed doors at a private meeting of ministers. Is this honest? I am afraid that it is with some as it was with the schoolmaster in one of the towns of a southern state in America. A grand old black preacher named Jasper had taught his people that the world is as flat as a pancake, and that the sun goes around it every day. We

> The way to peace is not in disguising convictions, but in the honest expression of them in the power of the Holy Spirit.

have not embraced this part of his teaching, but some people did, and one of them went to a schoolmaster with his boy and asked, "Do you teach the children that the world is round or flat?"

The schoolmaster cautiously answered, "Yes."

The inquirer was puzzled, so he asked for a clearer answer. "Do you teach your children that the world is round, or that the world is flat?"

Then the American schoolmaster answered, "That depends upon the opinions of the parents."

I suspect that even in Great Britain, in a few cases, a good deal depends upon the inclination of the leading deacon, or the principal tither, or the gilded youth in the congregation. If this is true, the crime is loathsome.

But whether it is for this or for any other cause that we teach with a divided tongue, the result will be highly damaging. I venture here to quote a story which I heard from our beloved brother Archibald Brown, to whom I referred earlier. A freeloader called upon a minister to try to get money from him. The good man did not like the beggar's appearance much, and he said to him, "I do not care for your case, and I see no special reason why you should come to me."

The beggar replied, "I am sure you would help me if you knew what great benefit I have received from your blessed ministry."

"What is that?" asked the pastor.

The beggar replied, "Why, sir, when I first came to hear you I cared neither for God nor devil, but now, under your ministry, I have come to love them both."

What a surprise if, under some teachers' deceitful talk, people grow to love both truth and falsehood! People will say, "We like this form of doctrine, and we like the other also."

The fact is, they would like anything if only a clever deceiver would present it to them in a believable way. They admire Moses and Aaron, but they would not say a word against Jannes and Jambres, the magicians who opposed them.[21] We will not join in any group which seems to aim at such an idea.

We must preach the gospel so distinctly that our people know what we are preaching. *For if the trumpet gives an uncertain sound, who shall prepare himself to the battle?* (1 Corinthians 14:8). Don't puzzle your people with doubtful speeches.

"Well," said someone, "I had a new idea the other day. I did not enlarge upon it; but I just tossed it out there."

That is a very good thing to do with most of your

---

21   2 Timothy 3:8, Exodus 7.

new ideas. Throw them out, by all means, but mind where you are when you do it, for if you throw them out from the pulpit, they may strike somebody and inflict a wound on faith. Throw out your whims, but first go alone in a boat a mile out to sea. Once you have thrown out your hasty trivial thoughts, leave them to the fishes.

Separating the Foxes from the Dogs

Nowadays, we have a class of people around us who preach Christ, and even preach the gospel, but then they preach a great deal else which is not true, and thus they destroy the good of all that they deliver, and lure men to error. They would be styled "evangelical" and yet be part of the school which is really anti-evangelical. Watch out for these people.

I have heard that a fox, when hunted closely by dogs, will pretend to be one of them, and run with the pack. That is what certain people are aiming for right now: the foxes would seem to be dogs. But in the case of the fox, his strong scent betrays him, and the dogs soon find him out, and even so, the scent of false doctrine is not easily concealed, and the game does not go on for long.

> We must preach the gospel so distinctly that our people know what we are preaching.

There are existing ministers who make it difficult to tell whether they are dogs or foxes, but all people will know our quality as long as we live, and they will not doubt what we believe and teach. We will not hesitate to speak in the strongest English words we can find, and in the plainest sentences we can put together, that which we hold as fundamental truth.

I have spent this much time on my first point, and the other two must, therefore, occupy less time, though I judge them to be of the first importance.

Now we must review our army.

Chapter 3

Our Army

What can individual men do in a great crusade? We are associated with all the people of the Lord. We need the members of our churches to be fellow soldiers; these must go out and win souls for Christ. We need the cooperation of the entire brotherhood. What is to be accomplished unless the saved ones go forth, all of them, for the salvation of others? But the question now is raised: is there to be a church at all?

Is there to be a distinct army of saints, or are we to include atheists? You have heard of "the church of the future,"[22] which we are to have instead of the church of Jesus Christ.[23] It has been suggested that in such a

---

22   It is likely Spurgeon was referring to controversial newspaper editor, William Thomas Stead (1849-1912), and British nonconformist minister and politician, John Clifford (1836-1923).

23   *Original footnote from Spurgeon's book:* At this point the audience could not be restrained, but stopped the speaker with cheers and laughter, to which he answered, "Nay, do not stop me in the middle of a sentence. My rule is not to mention names, and yet you have found a name hidden in a harmless word."

church – the "ideal church" of the future – all Christian distinction will cease, atheists will be welcomed, and the church itself will run a theatre and a pub.[24] Since its extreme groups will take in atheists, we may hope, in our charity, that it will include evil spirits also. What a wonderful church it will certainly be when we see it! It will be anything else you want to call it, but not a church.

When the soldiers of Christ will have included in their ranks all the outlaws of the opponent, will there be any army for Christ at all? Isn't it plainly a surrender at the very beginning of the war? That is what I make it out to be.

We must not only believe in the church of God, but also recognize it very distinctly. Some denominations recognize anything and everything more than the church. Such a thing as a meeting of the church is unknown. In some circles, "the church" signifies the ministers or clergy, but in truth, it should signify the whole body of the faithful, and there should be an opportunity for these to meet together to act as a church. It is the role of the church of God to carry on the work of God in the land. The final power and direction is with our Lord Jesus, and under Him it should stay, not with a few who are chosen by delegation or by voting, but with the whole body of believers.

> **It is the role of the church of God to carry on the work of God in the land.**

---

24   Found in *The Review of Reviews Volume 3* by William Thomas Stead, p. 156.

More and more, we must acknowledge the church which God has placed in our care, and in so doing, we will awaken a strength which otherwise has laid dormant. If the church is recognized by Christ Jesus, it is worthy to be recognized by us, for we are the servants of the church.

A Standard for Churches

Yes, we believe there ought to be a church. But churches are very disappointing things. Every pastor of a large church will attest to this. I do not know that the churches of today are any worse than they used to be in Paul's time, or any better. The churches at Corinth and Laodicea and other cities exhibited serious faults, and if there are faults in ours, we shouldn't be surprised; but yet we should grieve over such things and work toward a higher standard. Although we acknowledge the members of our church are not all they ought to be, neither are we ourselves. Yet, if I went looking for excellent company, I would certainly choose the members of my church. As the hymn says:

> "These are the company I keep:
> These are the choicest friends I know."[25]

O Jerusalem, with all thy faults, I love thee still![26] The people of God are still the aristocracy of the human race. God bless them! Yes, we intend to have a church.

Now, is that church to be real or statistical? That

---

25 A hymn by Isaac Watts based on and titled *Psalm 16*, 1806.

26 Modified from a quote by William Cowper that said, "England, with all thy faults, I love thee still – My country!"

depends very much on you, dear colleagues. I would urge you to resolve not to have a church unless it is a real one. Too often, religious statistics are shockingly false. Manufacturing false facts isn't unheard of in some circles, as we know. I heard of one case the other day where an increase of four attendees was reported, but had the attendance list been corrected at all, there was a decrease of twenty-five. Isn't it falsehood when numbers are manipulated? There is a way of making numbers add up as they should not add up. Never do this. Let's not keep names in our records when they are only names. Some of the good old people like to keep them there, and cannot bear to have them removed, but when you do not know where individuals are, nor what they are, how can you count them? They are gone to America, or to Australia, or to heaven, but as far as your list is concerned, they are with you still. Is this right?

It may not be possible to be absolutely accurate, but let's aim at it. We ought to see this in a very serious light and purge ourselves of the sin of false reporting, for God Himself will not bless mere names. It is not His way to work with those who act falsely. If there isn't a real person for each name, modify your list. Keep your church real and effective, or don't make a report. A merely nominal church is a lie. Let it be what it professes to be. We may not take delight in statistics, but we ought to know the facts.

Growing the Next-Generation Church

Is this church to increase, or is it to die out? It will do either one or the other. We will see our friends begin to pass away, and, if there are no young men and young women converted and brought in and added to us, the church on earth will have immigrated to the church triumphant above in heaven. And what should be done for the cause and the kingdom of the Master here on the earth below?

We should be crying, praying, and pleading that the church may continually grow. We must preach, visit, pray, and labor for this end. May the Lord add unto us daily such as are saved! If there is no harvest, can the seed be the true seed? Are we preaching apostolic doctrine if we never see apostolic results?

> If a church is to be what it ought to be for the purposes of God, we must train it in the holy art of prayer.

Oh, my brethren, our hearts should be ready to break if there is no increase in the flocks we tend. Oh Lord, we plead with you, send increase!

Praying Churches

If a church is to be what it ought to be for the purposes of God, we must train it in the holy art of prayer. Churches without prayer meetings are grievously common. Even if there was only one church without prayer meetings, it would be one to weep over. In many churches, the prayer meeting is only the skeleton of a gathering; the form is kept up, but the people do not come. There is no interest and no power in connection with the meeting.

Oh, my brothers, please don't let this be true with you! Do train the people to continually meet together for prayer. Move them to never-ending prayer. There is a holy art in it. Study to show yourselves approved by the prayerfulness of your people. If you pray yourself, you will want them to pray with you, and when they begin to pray with you, and for you, and for the work of the Lord, they will want more prayer themselves, and the appetite will grow. Believe me, if a church does not pray, it is dead. Instead of putting united prayer last, put it first. Everything will hinge upon the power of prayer in the church.

All of our churches ought to be busy for God. What is the use of a church that simply comes together to hear sermons, even as a family gathers to eat its meals? I ask, what is the profit, if it does no work? Aren't many professors sadly lazy in the Lord's work, though diligent enough in their own? Because of Christian idleness, we hear of the necessity for entertainment and all sorts of nonsense. If they were at work for the Lord Jesus, we would not hear of this.

A good woman said to a housewife, "Mrs. So-and-so, how do you manage to occupy yourself?"

"Why," she replied, "my dear, you see there are so many children that there is much work to be done in my house."

"Yes," said the other. "I see it. I see there is much work to be done in your house, but as it is never done, I was wondering how you occupied yourself."

Much needs to be done by a Christian church within its own bounds, and for the neighborhood, and for the poor and the fallen, and for the heathen world, and so forth. And if it is well attended to, then minds and hearts and hands and tongues will be occupied, and they will not ask for diversions. Let idleness come in and that spirit which rules lazy people, and a desire to be amused will arise. What amusements they are too! If religion is not a comedy show with some congregations, at any rate more people come out to see a comedy than to unite in prayer. I cannot understand it. The man who is all aglow with love for Jesus finds little need for amusement. He has no time for unimportant things. He is exceptionally motivated to save souls, and establish the truth, and enlarge the kingdom of his Lord.

> **The man who is all aglow with love for Jesus finds little need for amusement.**

There has always been some unrelenting call for the cause of God on me, and, once determined, there has been another, and another, and another, and the scramble has been to find opportunity to do the work that must be done. Therefore, I have not had the time for gallivanting overseas after trivial things. Oh, to get a working church! The German churches, when our dear friend Mr. Oncken[27] was alive, always carried out the rule of asking every member, "What are you going to do for Christ?" and they put the answer down in a book. The one thing that was required of every member was that he or she should continue doing something for the Savior. If he stopped doing anything, it became a matter for church discipline, because he was an idle professor of faith, and could not be allowed to remain

---

27 Johann Gerhard Oncken (1800-1884), a pioneer German Baptist preacher.

in the church like a drone in a hive of working bees. He must do or go.

Healthy Churches

Oh, for a vineyard without an unfruitful fig tree to obstruct the ground! At present, most of our sacred warfare is carried on by a small body of intensely living, earnest people, and the rest are either in the hospital or are nothing but camp followers. We are thankful for that consecrated few, but we hunger to see the altar fire consuming all that is supposedly laid upon the altar.

Brothers, we want churches that also produce saints, people of mighty faith and prevalent prayer, people of holy living, and of consecrated giving, people filled with the Holy Spirit. We must have these saints as rich clusters of fruit, or surely, we are not branches of the true Vine. I would love to see in every church a Mary sitting at Jesus's feet, a Martha serving Jesus, a Peter, and a John. But the best name we can come up with for a church is "All Saints"? All believers should be saints, and all may be saints.

We have no connection with "the latter-day saints,"[28] but we love everyday saints. Oh, for more of them! If God will help in such a way that each person in the whole congregation of the faithful will individually come to full maturity in Christ Jesus, then we will see greater things than these. Glorious times will come when believers have glorious character.

We also want churches that know the truth and

---

28   Mostly likely referring to The Church of Jesus Christ of Latter-day Saints.

are well taught in the things of God. What do some Christian people know? They come and hear, and, in the plenitude of your wisdom, you instruct them, but how little they receive to store up for teaching others! Brothers, the fault lies partly with us and partly with themselves. If we taught better, they would learn better. Notice how little many professors know – not enough to give them discernment between living truth and deadly error. Old-fashioned believers could give you chapter and verse for what they believed, but how few of this type remain!

> Glorious times will come when believers have glorious character.

Our esteemed grandfathers were comfortable with discussing "the covenants." I love people who love the covenant of grace, and base their theology on it; the doctrine of the covenants is the key of theology. Those who feared the Lord spoke often to one another. They used to speak of everlasting life and all that comes from it. They had a good argument for this belief and an excellent reason for that other doctrine, and to try to shake them was by no means easy. You might as well have hoped to shake the pillars of the universe, for they were steadfast and could not be tossed about with every wind of doctrine. They knew what they knew, and they held fast to that which they had learned.

What is to become of our country, with the present deluge of Romanism pouring upon us through the Ritualistic party, unless our churches abound in firm believers who can discern between the regeneration of the Holy Spirit and its ceremonial substitute?[29] What is to become of our churches in this day of skepticism, when people point at every fixed truth with the finger of doubt, unless our people have the truths of the gospel written in their hearts? Oh, for a church of outright believers who are resistant to the soul-destroying doubt which pours upon us in showers!

Yet all this would not reach our ideal. We want a church of a missionary character, which will go forward to gather up people for God from all parts of the world. A church is a soul-saving organization, or it is nothing. If the salt provides no preserving influence on what is around it, what is the use of it? Yet some hold back from effort in their own neighbor-hoods because of the poverty and immorality of the people. I remember a minister who is now deceased – a very good man he was too, in many respects – but he utterly amazed me with a reply he made to a question of mine. I commented that he had an awful neighbor-hood around his church, and I said, "Are you able to do much for them?"

> A church is a soul-saving organization, or it is nothing.

He answered, "No. I feel almost glad that we keep clear of them, for, you see, if any of them were converted, it would be a terrible burden upon us."

I knew him to be a person of caution and prudence, but this surprised me, and I wanted an explanation.

"Well," he said, "we would have to support them;

---

29 Spurgeon's reference to the Ritualistic party most likely included Roman Catholics, who emphasized the rituals and liturgical ceremony of the church, in particular, Holy Communion.

they are mostly thieves and prostitutes, and if converted they would have no means of making a living, and we are a poor people, and could not provide for them."

He was a devout man, and it was to a person's benefit to have a conversation with him. And yet, that was how he had gradually come to look at the case. His people had a difficult time keeping up with the expenses of the church, and thus the chill of poverty suppressed his compassionate fire and froze the warm and hospitable river of his soul. There was a great deal of common sense in what he said, but yet it was an awful thing to say it, and certainly not biblical. We don't want to be worshipers who forever sing:

> "We are a garden walled around,
>   Chosen and made peculiar ground;
> A little spot enclosed by grace,
>   Out of the world's wild wilderness."[30]

It's a good song for occasional singing, but not when it comes to mean "We are very few, and we wish to be."

No, no, brothers! We are a little detachment of the King's soldiers stationed in a foreign country upon soldier guard duty, yet our goal isn't only to hold the fort, but also to add territory to our Lord's dominion. We are not to be driven out, but on the contrary, we are going to drive out the Canaanites, for this land belongs to us; it is given to us of the Lord, and we will subdue it. May we be ablaze with the spirit of discoverers and

---

30   "We Are a Garden Walled Around" by Isaac Watts (1674-1748).

conquerors, and never rest while there remains a group to be rescued or a territory to be evangelized!

Our Mission

We are rowing like men in a lifeboat on a stormy sea, and we are hurrying to a shipwreck in the distance where people are drowning. If we can't bring that old wreck to shore, we will, at least, by the power of God, rescue those who would otherwise die, save lives, and bring the redeemed to the shores of salvation.

Our mission, like our Lord's, is to gather out the chosen of God from among men, so they may live to the glory of God. Every saved man should be – under God – a savior, and the church is not in a right state until she has reached that concept of herself. The elect church is saved so she may save, cleansed so she may cleanse, blessed so she may bless. All the world is the field, and all the members of the church should work there for the great farmer. Wastelands are to be reclaimed, and forests broken up by the plow, until the barren place begins to blossom as the rose. We must not be content with holding our own; we must invade the territories of the Prince of Darkness.

> We must not be content with holding our own; we must invade the territories of the Prince of Darkness.

My brothers, what is our relation to this church? What is our position in it? We are servants. May we always know our place and keep it! The highest place in the church will always come to the one who willingly chooses the lowest, while the one who aspires to be great among his comrades will sink to be least of all. Certain people might have been something if they had not thought themselves to be something. A consciously great man is an obviously little one. A lord over God's heritage is a lower-class usurper without a right to the position. The one who is always ready to serve the very least of the family in his or her heart and soul, who expects to be taken advantage of, and willingly sacrifices reputation and friendship for Christ's sake, is the one who will fulfill a heaven-sent ministry. We are not sent to be ministered to, but to minister. Let's sing unto our Well-Beloved:

> "There's not a lamb in all thy flock,
>   I would disdain to feed;
> There's not a foe before whose face
>   I'd fear thy cause to plead."[31]

The Role of Leaders

We must also be examples to the flock. The one who cannot be safely imitated ought not to be tolerated in a pulpit.

Did I hear of a minister who was always arguing for preeminence? Or of another who was mean and covetous? Or of a third whose conversation was not always pure? Or of a fourth who did not rise, as a rule, until eleven o'clock in the morning? I would hope that this last rumor was altogether false. An idle minister – what will become of him? A pastor who neglects his office? Does he expect to go to heaven?

---

31   Philip Doddridge

I was about to say, "If he does go there at all, may it be soon." A lazy minister is a creature despised by men and abhorred by God. "You give your minister only fifty pounds a year," I said to a farmer. [32] "Why, the poor man cannot live on it."

The answer was, "Look here, sir! I tell you what. We give him a good deal more than he earns."

It is a sad pity when that can be said; it is an injury to all those who follow our sacred calling. We are to be examples to our flock in all things. In all diligence, in all gentleness, in all humility, and in all holiness, we are to excel. When Caesar went on his wars, one thing always helped his soldiers to bear hardships: they knew Caesar experienced whatever they experienced. He marched if they marched, he thirsted if they thirsted, and he was always in the heat of the battle if they were fighting.

We must do more than others if we are officers in Christ's army. We must not cry, "Go on!" but instead cry, "*Come* on!" Our people may reasonably expect of us, at the very least, that we should be among the most self-denying, the most hardest-working, and the most sincere in the church, and somewhat more. We cannot expect to see holy churches if those of us who are supposed to be their examples are unsanctified. If there is, in any of our colleagues, consecration and sanctification evident to all people, God has blessed them, and God will bless them more and more. If these are lacking in us, we do not need to search far to find the cause of our lack of success.

---

32   Equivalent of three or four dollars in the late 1800s.

I have many things to say to you, but you cannot endure them now, because the time is long and you are weary. I desire, however, if you can gather up your patience and your strength, to dwell for a little on the most important part of my three subjects. Allow me to pray here for the help of the One whose name and person I would magnify.

Come, Holy Spirit, heavenly dove, and rest upon us now!

Chapter 4

Our Strength

Assuming we preach the Word alone, assuming we are surrounded by a model church – which, sadly, is not always the case, but assuming it is so – our strength is the next consideration. This must come from the Spirit of God. We believe in the Holy Spirit, and in our absolute dependence on Him. We believe, but do we believe practically? Brothers, as to ourselves and our own work, do we believe in the Holy Spirit? Do we believe because we habitually prove the truth of the doctrine?

We must depend upon the Spirit in our preparations. Is this true with us all? Are you in the habit of working your way into the meaning of texts by the guidance of the Holy Spirit? Every man that goes to the land of heavenly knowledge must work his route toward that place, but he must work out his course in the strength of the Holy Spirit, or he will arrive at some island in the sea of fancy, and never set his foot upon the sacred shores of the truth.

You do not know the truth, my brother, because you have read Hodge's *Outlines of Theology*, or Fuller's *The Gospel Worthy of All Acceptation*, or Owen's *On the Spirit*,[33] or any other classic of our faith. You do not know the truth, my brother, merely because you accept the Westminster Assembly's Confession of Faith and have studied it perfectly. No, we know nothing until we are taught of the Holy Spirit, who speaks to the heart, rather than to the ear.

We must depend upon the Holy Spirit.

It is a wonderful fact that we do not even hear the voice of Jesus until the Spirit rests upon us. John says, *I was in the Spirit in the day of the Lord and heard behind me a great voice as of a trumpet* (Revelation 1:10). He did not hear that voice until he was in the Spirit. How many heavenly words we miss because we do not abide in the Spirit!

We cannot succeed in supplication unless the Holy Spirit helps our weaknesses, for true prayer is "praying in the Holy Spirit." The Spirit makes an atmosphere around every living prayer, and within that circle, prayer lives and reigns; outside of it, prayer is a dead formality. As to ourselves, then, in our study, in prayer, in thought, in word, and in deed, we must depend upon the Holy Spirit.

---

33 Archibald Alexander Hodge (1823-1886), Andrew Fuller (1754-1815), John Owen (1616-1683).

The Power of the Spirit

In the pulpit do we really and truly rest on the aid of the Spirit? I do not judge any brother for his mode of preaching, but I must confess that it seems very odd to me when a brother prays that the Holy Spirit may help him in preaching, and then I see him put his hand behind him and he pulls a manuscript out of his pocket – so fashioned that he can place it in the middle of his Bible, and read from it without being suspected of doing so.

These precautions for ensuring secrecy look as though the man was a little ashamed of his paper, but I think he should be far more ashamed of his precautions. Does he expect the Spirit of God to bless him while he is practicing a trick? And how can the Spirit help him when he reads from a paper, from which anyone else might read without the Spirit's aid? What does the Holy Spirit have to do with the business? Truly, He may have had something to do with the manuscript in the composing of it, but in the pulpit, His aid is unnecessary.

The more honest thing to do would be to thank the Lord for the assistance provided, and ask that the message the Spirit has enabled the preacher to get into his pocket may now enter the people's hearts. Still, if the Holy Spirit should have anything to say to the people that is not in the paper, how can He say it through us? He seems to me to be effectively blocked as to freshness of speech by that method of ministry. Still, it is not for me to judge, although I may quietly beg for freedom in prophesying, and ask us to leave room for the Lord to give us words to say at the moment we get up to speak.

Furthermore, we must depend upon the Spirit of God when it comes to our results. No person among us really thinks that he could regenerate a soul. We are not so foolish as to claim power to change a heart of stone. We may not dare to presume quite that far, and yet we may come to think that by our experience, we can help people get through spiritual difficulties. Can we?

We may be hopeful that our enthusiasm will push the living church before us and drag the dead world after us. Will it be so? Perhaps we imagine that if we could only get a revival started, we should easily be able to ensure large additions to the church. Is it worthwhile to *start up* a revival? Aren't all true revivals to be *brought down*?

We must depend upon the Spirit of God when it comes to our results.

We may persuade ourselves that drums and trumpets and shouting will do a great deal. But, my comrades, "the Lord is not in the wind."[34] Results worth having come from that silent but omnipotent Worker whose name is the Spirit of God. In Him, and in Him only, must we trust for the conversion of a single Sunday-school child, and for every genuine revival. We must look to Him to keep our people together, and to build them up into a holy temple. We must look to Him. The Spirit might say, even as our Lord did, "Without me, you can do nothing."

What is the church of God without the Holy Spirit? Ask, what would Hermon be without its dew,[35] or Egypt

---

34   From Elijah's story in 1 Kings 19.

35   A reference to Psalm 133:3.

without its Nile? Remember the land of Canaan when the curse of Elijah fell upon it. For three years it didn't have either dew or rain.

This is how Christendom would become without the Spirit. What the valleys would be without their brooks, or the cities without their wells; what the cornfields would be without the sun, or the vintage without the summer – that would be our churches without the Spirit. Think also of day without light, or life without breath, or heaven without God, as of Christian service without the Holy Spirit.

Nothing can supply His place if He is absent; the pastures are a desert, the fruitful fields are a wilderness, the fertile plains of Sharon deteriorate, and the beautifully wooded mountain range of Carmel is burned with fire.

We pray, blessed Spirit of the Lord, forgive us because we have done you such outrage by our forgetfulness of you, by our proud self-sufficiency, by resisting your influences, and by quenching your fire! From this point forward, work in us according to your own excellence. Make our hearts tenderly impressible, and then turn us as sealing wax on a document, and stamp upon us the image of the Son of God.

With this prayer and confession of faith, let's pursue our speaking and teaching topics in the power of the good Spirit about whom we speak.

What the Spirit Does

What does the Holy Spirit do? Beloved, is there any good work that He does not do? It is His role to activate and stir up hearts, to convince, to illuminate, to cleanse, to guide, to preserve, to console, to confirm, to perfect, and to use. We could say so much under each one of these subheadings!

He is the one who works in us to will and to do. God is the one who has brought about all things. Glory be unto the Holy Spirit for all He has accomplished in such poor, imperfect natures as ours! We can do nothing apart from the life-giving sap which flows to us from Jesus the Vine. Our own ability is suitable only to cause us shame. We never go a step toward heaven without the Holy Spirit. We never lead another on the heavenward road without the Holy Spirit. We have no acceptable thought, or word, or deed, apart from the Holy Spirit. Even lifting up one's eyes toward heaven in hope, or the sudden prayer of the heart's desire, must be His work. All good things are of Him and through Him, from beginning to end. There is no fear of exaggerating here. Do we, however, apply this conviction to our real-life actions?

Instead of expanding on what the Spirit of God does, let me refer to your experience, and ask you a question or two. Do you remember times when the Spirit of God has been graciously present in fullness of power with you and with your people? What seasons those have been! That Sabbath was a great day, a spiritual high. Those services were like the worship of Jacob when he said, "Surely, God was in this place!"

So much mutual nonverbal communication goes on between the preacher in the Spirit and the people in the Spirit! Their eyes seem to talk to us as much as our tongues talk to them. Then, they are a very different people from what they are on common occasions; there is even a beauty upon their faces while we are glorifying the Lord Jesus, and they enjoy and drink in our testimony.

Our Motive in Teaching

Have you ever seen a gentleman of the modern school enjoying his own preaching? Our evangelical preachers are very happy in delivering what our liberal friends are pleased to call their "platitudes," but the moderns in their wisdom feel no such joy.

Can you imagine a naysayer in the motivational, emotional glow which our Welsh friends call the *hwyl*?[36] How grimly cynics talk at length about the post-exilic theory! They remind me of Ruskin's expression: "Turner had no joy of his mill." I grant you, there is nothing to enjoy, and they are evidently glad to get through their task of piling up meatless bones. They stand at an empty feed trough, amusing themselves by chewing on the empty container. They get through their preaching, and they are fairly lifeless until Monday comes with a football game, or a musical at the schoolhouse, or a political meeting.

To them, preaching is work, though they don't put much work into it. The old preachers, and some of those who now live but are said to be out-of-date, think of the pulpit as a throne, or a triumphal chariot, and are near heaven when the Spirit helps them preach with power.

---

36 *English Oxford Dictionary*: "a stirring feeling of emotional motivation and energy."

Poor fools that we are, preaching our "antiquated" gospel! We do enjoy the task. Our gloomy doctrines make us very happy. Strange, isn't it? The gospel is evidently marrow and fatness to us, and our beliefs – albeit, of course, they are very absurd and unphilosophical – do make us content, and make us very confident and happy.

I may say of some of my brethren that their very eyes seem to sparkle, and their souls seem to glow, while elaborating about free grace and dying love. It is true, friends, that when we have the presence of God, then we and our hearers are carried away with heavenly delight. That isn't all. When the Spirit of God is present, every saint loves his fellow saint, and there is no fighting among us unless it is fighting about who is the most loving. Then prayer fights and wins, and ministry sows good seed and reaps large sheaves. Then conversions are plentiful, restorations are abundant, and advances in grace are seen on every side. Hallelujah! With the Spirit of God all goes well.

The Life in Our Message

But do you know the opposite condition? I hope you do not. It is death in life. I trust you have never, in your scientific experiments, been cruel enough to put a mouse in an air pump, and gradually let the air out until there was nothing but a vacuum left. I have read of the fatal experiment. Oh, the poor mouse! As the air gets thinner and thinner, he suffers greatly, and when it is all gone, there he lies – dead. Have you never yourself been in a vacuum spiritually? You have only been there long enough to perceive that the sooner you escaped, the better for you.

Someone said to me the other day, "Well, as to the sermon which I heard from the modern-thought theologian, there was no great harm in it, for on this occasion he kept clear of false doctrine. But the whole affair was so intensely cold. I felt like a man who has fallen down a crevasse in a glacier, and I felt shut up as if I could not breathe the air of heaven."

You know that arctic cold, and it may occasionally be felt even where the doctrine is sound. When the Spirit of God is gone, even truth itself becomes an iceberg. How worthless religion is when it is frozen and lifeless! The Holy Spirit has gone, and all energy and enthusiasm have gone with Him. The scene becomes like that described by Samuel Taylor Coleridge in *The Rime of the Ancient Mariner*, when the ship was marooned:

> "The very deep did rot,
>   Alas, that ever this should be!
> Yea, slimy things did crawl with legs
>   Upon the slimy sea.
> Within the ship all was death."

And we have seen it this way within a church. I am tempted to apply Coleridge's lines to much that we see in those churches which deserve the name of "congregations of the dead." He describes how the bodies of the dead were inspired and the ship moved on, each dead man fulfilling his responsibility in a dead and formal fashion:

"The helmsman steered, the ship moved on;
    Yet never a breeze up blew;
The mariners all 'gan work the ropes,
    Where they were wont to do;
They raised their limbs like lifeless tools
    We were a ghastly crew."

All living fellowship was lacking, for the Ancient Mariner says:

"The body of my brother's son
    Stood by me, knee to knee:
The body and I pulled at one rope,
    But he said naught to me."

It is so similar in those "respectable" congregations where people don't know one another, and a dignified seclusion takes the place of all holy fellowship. To the preacher, if he is the only living man in the congregation, the church provides very dreary companionship. His sermons fall on ears that don't hear them properly.

"'Twas night, calm night, the moon was high;
    The dead men stood together.
All stood together on the deck
    For a charnel-dungeon fitter:
All fixed on me their stony eyes,
    That in the moon did glitter."

Yes, the preacher's moonlight – cold and cheerless – falls on faces which are like it. The sermon impresses their emotionless minds and fixes their stony eyes – as Coleridge put it in his poem – but hearts, well, hearts are not in fashion in those regions. Hearts are for the realm of life, but without the Holy Spirit, what do congregations know of true life?

If the Holy Spirit has gone, death reigns, and the church is a tomb. Therefore, we must beg Him to abide with us, and we must never rest until He does so. Oh friends, please don't let it be that I talk to you about this and then we permit the matter to drop. Instead, let's each one with heart and soul seek to have the power of the Holy Spirit abiding on us.

Have we received the Holy Spirit? Is He with us now? If He is, how can we secure His future presence? How can we coerce Him to abide with us?

The Presence of the Holy Spirit

I would say, first, to treat Him as He should be treated. Worship Him as the Lord God who is worthy of divine worship. Never call the Holy Spirit an "it," nor speak of Him as if He were a doctrine, or an influence, or an orthodox myth. Reverence Him, love Him, and trust Him with familiar yet reverent confidence. He is God; let Him be God to you.

See to it that you act in compliance with His working. The mariner to the east cannot create the winds at his will, but he knows when the trade winds blow, and he takes advantage of the season to speed his vessel. Put out to sea in holy initiative when the heavenly wind is with you. Take the sacred tide at its flood. Increase your meetings when you feel that the Spirit of God is blessing them. Press home the truth more earnestly than ever when the Lord is opening ears and hearts to accept it.

You will soon know when there is anointing like dew around you; prize the gracious visitation. The farmer says, "Make hay while the sun shines." You cannot make the sun shine; that is quite out of your power, but you can use the sun while it shines. *And when thou hearest thunder going through the tops of the mulberry trees, then thou shalt move* (2 Samuel 5:24). Be hardworking in season and out of season, but in a growing season work twice as hard.

> Be hardworking in season and out of season, but in a growing season work twice as hard.

Always, in beginning, in continuing, and in ending any and every good work, consciously and in very truth depend upon the Holy Spirit. He must even give you a sense of your need for Him, and the prayers where you ask Him to come must come from Him. You are engaged in a work that is so spiritual – so far above all human power – that to forget the Spirit is to ensure defeat. Make the Holy Spirit to be the *sine qua non* – the essential part – of your efforts, and go so far as to say to Him, "If your presence does not go with us, do not move us from this place."

Rest only in Him and then reserve all the glory for Him. Be especially mindful of this, for this is a tender point with Him; He will not give His glory to another. Remember to praise the Spirit of God from your inmost heart, and be in grateful awe that He would stoop low enough to work through you. Please Him by glorifying Christ. Give Him reverence by yielding yourself to His impulses, and by hating everything that grieves Him. The consecration of your whole being will be the best psalm to His praise.

A Call to Holiness

There are a few more things that I want you to know, and then I will be done. Remember that the Holy Spirit has His ways and methods, and there are some things which He will not do. You should know He makes no promise to bless compromises. If we make an agreement with error or sin, we do it at our own risk. If we do anything that we are not clear about, if we tamper with truth or holiness, if we are friends with the world, if we make provision for the human nature, if we preach halfheartedly and collaborate with those who hold wrong beliefs, we have no promise that the Holy Spirit will go with us.

The great promise runs in quite another strain:

> *Therefore come out from among them, and be ye separate, saith the Lord, and do not touch the unclean thing; and I will receive you and will be a Father unto you, and ye shall be my sons and daughters, saith the Lord Almighty* (2 Corinthians 6:17-18).

This passage is the only place in the New Testament, with the exception of the book of Revelation, where God is called by the name of the Lord Almighty. If you want to know what great things God can do as the Lord Almighty, be separate from the world and from those who desert the truth. The title *Lord Almighty* is evidently quoted from the Old Testament. He is *El Shaddai*, God all-sufficient, the many-breasted[37] God. We will never know the utmost power of God for supplying all our needs until we have cut our connection once and for all with everything that does not align with His thinking.

Avoid the Appearance of Evil

Was it Abraham who said to the king of Sodom, "I will not take from you *a goodly Babylonish garment and two hundred shekels of silver and a wedge of gold of fifty shekels weight*"?[38]

No, no. Abraham said, *I have lifted up my hand unto the LORD, the most high God, the possessor of the heavens and of the earth, that I will not take from a thread even to a shoelatchet; I will not take any thing that is thine, lest thou should say, I have made Abram rich* (Genesis 14:22-23).

That was "the cut direct" – a refusal to even look at the evil option. The man of God will have nothing to do with Sodom, or with false doctrine. If you see anything that is evil, give it the cut direct. Have nothing to do with those who have nothing to do with truth. Then you will be prepared to receive the promise, and not until then.

Dear friends, remember that wherever there is great

---

37 Another view of the term, which saw it as related to fertility and blessings.

38 Referring to Achan who stole plunder from the Lord in Joshua 7:21.

love, there is sure to be great jealousy. *Love is strong as death.* What next? *Jealousy is hard as Sheol* – as cruel as the grave (Song of Solomon 8:6). *God is love* (1 John 4:8 KJV), and for that very reason, *the LORD thy God is a jealous God among you* (Deuteronomy 6:15). Keep clear of everything that makes you unclean, or that would grieve the Holy Spirit. For if He is displeased with us, we will soon be put to shame before the Enemy.

Brave Warriors of Faith

Next, note that He makes no promise to cowardice. If you allow the fear of man to rule you, and wish to save yourself from suffering or ridicule, you will find little comfort in the promise of God. *Whosoever desires to save his life shall lose it* (Matthew 16:25). The promises of the Holy Spirit to us in our warfare are to those who are brave and strong, and by faith are made courageous in the moment of battle.[39]

If you allow the fear of man to rule you, and wish to save yourself from suffering or ridicule, you will find little comfort in the promise of God.

I wish that we would come to the place where we utterly despise ridicule and slander. If only we could have the self-oblivion of the Italian martyr about whom John Foxe speaks in his *Foxe's Book of Martyrs*! They condemned him to be burned alive, and he listened calmly to the sentence. But you know, burning martyrs – however delightful – is also expensive, and the mayor of the town did not care to pay for the firewood. And the

---

39   Concept taken from 1 Corinthians 16:13.

priests who had accused him also wanted to do the deed without personal expense.

They had an angry quarrel, and there stood the poor man, for whose benefit this kindling was to be contributed, quietly listening to their mutual accusations. When they found they could not settle the dispute, he said, "Gentlemen, I will end your dispute. It is a pity that either of you should be at so much expense to find firewood for my burning, and, for my Lord's sake, I will even pay for the wood that burns me, if you would like."

There is a fine touch of scorn as well as meekness there. I do not know that I would have paid that bill, but I have felt motivated to go a little out of the way to help the enemies of the truth to find fuel for their criticisms of me. Yes, yes! I will make me seem even more wicked and give them more to complain about. I will go through with the controversy for Christ's sake, and do nothing at all to quiet their anger.

Friends, if you compromise a little, if you try to save a little of your reputation with the people who abandon the truth, it will not go well with you. The one who is ashamed of Christ and His Word in this evil generation will find Christ is ashamed of him at the judgement.

The Spirit is Truth

I will be very brief on these points. Remember, next, that the Holy Spirit will never give approval for falsehood. Never! If what you preach is not the truth, God will not own it. Make sure of this.

In addition, the Holy Spirit never puts His signature

on a blank document. That would be unwise on the part of man, and the holy Lord will not commit such a foolish act. If we do not speak clear doctrine with plainness of speech, the Holy Spirit will not put His signature to our empty babbling. If we do not speak distinctly about Christ and His death and resurrection, we may say good-bye to true success.

Next, remember the Holy Spirit will never approve of sin, and to bless the ministry of some men would be to condone their evil ways. *Be ye clean, that bear the vessels of the LORD* (Isaiah 52:11). Let your character match your teaching, and let your churches be purged from open wrongdoers, in case the Holy Spirit would reject your teaching – not for its own sake, but because of the unpleasant taste of unholy living which dishonors it.

Remember, again, He will never encourage idleness. The Holy Spirit will not come in to rescue us from the consequences of willful neglect of the Word of God and study. If we allow ourselves to go about living all week doing nothing, we may not climb the pulpit stairs and dream that the Lord will be there and then tell us what to speak. If help were promised to this type of person, then the lazier the man, the better the sermon. If the Holy Spirit worked only by impromptu speakers, the less we would read our Bibles and the less we meditated on them the better.

If it is wrong to quote from books, "attention to reading" would not have been commanded. All this is obviously absurd, and not one of you will fall into such a delusion. We are compelled to spend much time in meditation, and give ourselves wholly to the Word of God and prayer, and when we have paid attention to these things, we may look for the Spirit's approval and cooperation. We ought to prepare the sermon as if all depended on us, and then we are to trust the Spirit of God, knowing that all depends on Him. The Holy Spirit sends no one into the harvest to sleep among the haystacks, but to bear the work and heat of the day. We should pray to ask God to send more "laborers" into the vineyard, for the Spirit will be with the strength of laborers, but He will not be the friend of loiterers.

Be Humble

I remind you, the Holy Spirit will not bless us in order to sustain our pride. Isn't it possible that we may wish for a great blessing so others might think of us as great? This will hinder our success. When the string of the hunter's bow is out of tune, the arrow will shoot crooked. What does God do with men who are proud? Does He exalt them? I believe not.

Herod made an eloquent speech, and he put on a dazzling silver robe, which glistened in the sun, and when the people saw his robes and listened to his charming voice, they cried, "It is the voice of a god, and not of a man!"

But the Lord struck him down, and worms ate him (in Acts 12:23). Worms have a strict right to claim proud flesh, and when we get very mighty and very big, the worms expect to make a meal of us. *Pride goes before destruction, and a haughty spirit before a fall* (Proverbs 16:18).

Keep humble if you would have the Spirit of God

with you. The Holy Spirit takes no pleasure in the inflated discussion of the proud; how can He? Would you have Him support empty talk? *Humble thyself to walk with thy God* (Micah 6:8), oh preacher! For you cannot walk with Him in any other way. And if you do not walk with Him, your walking will be useless.

Live Peacefully

Consider again that the Holy Spirit will not dwell where there is conflict. Let's pursue peace with all men, and especially let's keep peace in our churches. Some of you are not yet blessed with this favor, and it might not be your fault. You have inherited old quarrels. In many small communities, all the members of the congregation are cousins to one another, and relatives usually agree to disagree. When cousins deceive their cousins, the seeds of ill will are sown, and these weeds invade even church life. Your predecessor's domineering in the past may have produced a good deal of quarrelling to last for many years to come. He was a man of war from his youth, and even when he is gone, the spirits which he called from out of the deep remain to haunt the spot.

We ought to prepare the sermon as if all depended on us, and then we are to trust the Spirit of God, knowing that all depends on Him.

I fear you cannot expect much blessing, for the Holy Dove does not dwell by troubled waters; He chooses to come where brotherly love continues. For great doctrines and matters of holy discipline, we may risk peace itself, but for ourselves or our comrades, I hope such conduct is far from us.

A Clear Purpose

Lastly, remember the Holy Spirit will only bless in alignment with His own established purpose. Our Lord explains what that purpose is: "*He* shall glorify me." He has come forward for this grand finale, and He will not put up with anything short of it. If, then, we do not preach Christ, what is the Holy Spirit to do with our preaching?

If we do not make the Lord Jesus glorious, if we do not lift Him high in the opinion of people, if we do not labor to make Him King of Kings and Lord of Lords, we will not have the Holy Spirit with us. Rhetoric, music, architecture, energy, and social status will be senseless if our one design is not to magnify the Lord Jesus, and we will work alone and work for nothing.

Conclusion

This is *all* that I have to say to you at this time. But, my dear friends, it is a great "*all*" if you first consider what I have to say, and then carry it out. May it have a practical effect on us! It will, if the great Worker uses it, and not otherwise.

Go forth, oh, soldiers of Jesus Christ, with *the sword of the Spirit, which is the word of God* (Ephesians 6:17). Go forth with the armies of the godly whom you lead, and let every person be strong in the Lord and in the power of His might. As people who came back to life from death, go forth in the reviving power of the Holy Spirit; you have no other strength.

May the blessing of the triune God rest on you, one and all, for the Lord Jesus Christ's sake!

Amen.

Charles Spurgeon – A Brief Biography

Charles Haddon Spurgeon was born on June 19, 1834, in Kelvedon, Essex, England. He was one of seventeen children in his family (nine of whom died in infancy). His father and grandfather were Nonconformist ministers in England. Due to economic difficulties, eighteen-month-old Charles was sent to live with his grandfather, who helped teach Charles the ways of God. Later in life, Charles remembered looking at the pictures in *Pilgrim's Progress* and in *Foxe's Book of Martyrs* as a young boy.

Charles did not have much of a formal education and never went to college. He read much throughout his life though, especially books by Puritan authors.

Even with godly parents and grandparents, young Charles resisted giving in to God. It was not until he was fifteen years old that he was born again. He was on his way to his usual church, but when a heavy snowstorm prevented him from getting there, he turned in at a little Primitive Methodist chapel. Though there were only about fifteen people in attendance, the preacher spoke from Isaiah 45:22: *Look unto me, and be ye saved, all the ends of the earth.* Charles Spurgeon's eyes were opened and the Lord converted his soul.

He began attending a Baptist church and teaching Sunday school. He soon preached his first sermon, and then when he was sixteen years old, he became the pastor of a small Baptist church in Cambridge. The church soon grew to over four hundred people, and Charles Spurgeon, at the age of nineteen, moved on to become the pastor of the New Park Street Church in London. The church grew from a few hundred attenders to a few thousand. They built an addition to the church, but still needed more room to accommodate the congregation. The Metropolitan Tabernacle was built in London in 1861, seating more than 5,000 people. Pastor Spurgeon preached the simple message of the cross, and thereby attracted many people who wanted to hear God's Word preached in the power of the Holy Spirit.

On January 9, 1856, Charles married Susannah Thompson. They had twin boys, Charles and Thomas. Charles and Susannah loved each other deeply, even amidst the difficulties and troubles that they faced in life, including health problems. They helped each other spiritually, and often together read the writings of Jonathan Edwards, Richard Baxter, and other Puritan writers.

Charles Spurgeon was a friend of all Christians, but he stood firmly on the Scriptures, and it didn't please all who heard him. Spurgeon believed in and preached on the sovereignty of God, heaven and hell, repentance, revival, holiness, salvation through Jesus Christ alone, and the infallibility and necessity of the Word of God. He spoke against worldliness and hypocrisy among Christians, and against Roman Catholicism, ritualism, and modernism.

One of the biggest controversies in his life was known as the "Down-Grade Controversy." Charles Spurgeon believed that some pastors of his time were "down-grading" the faith by compromising with the world or the new ideas of the age. He said that some pastors were denying the inspiration of the Bible, salvation by faith alone, and the truth of the Bible in other areas, such as creation. Many pastors who believed what Spurgeon condemned were not happy about this, and Spurgeon eventually resigned from the Baptist Union.

Despite some difficulties, Spurgeon became known as the "Prince of Preachers." He opposed slavery, started a pastors' college, opened an orphanage, led in helping feed and clothe the poor, had a book fund for pastors who could not afford books, and more.

Charles Spurgeon remains one of the most published preachers in history. His sermons were printed each week (even in the newspapers), and then the sermons for the year were re-issued as a book at the end of the year. The first six volumes, from 1855-1860, are known as *The Park Street Pulpit*, while the next fifty-seven volumes, from 1861-1917 (his sermons continued to be published long after his death), are known as *The Metropolitan Tabernacle Pulpit*. He also oversaw a monthly magazine-type publication called *The Sword and the Trowel,* and Spurgeon wrote many books, including *Lectures to My Students*, *All of Grace*, *Around the Wicket Gate*, *Advice for Seekers*, *John Ploughman's Talks*, *The Soul Winner*, *Words of Counsel for Christian Workers*, *Cheque Book of the Bank of Faith*, *Morning and Evening*, his autobiography, and more, including some commentaries, such as his twenty-year study on the Psalms – *The Treasury of David.*

Charles Spurgeon often preached ten times a week, preaching to an estimated ten million people during his lifetime. He usually preached from only one page of notes, and often from just an outline. He read about six books each week. During his lifetime, he had read *The Pilgrim's Progress* through more than one hundred times. When he died, his personal library consisted of more than 12,000 books. However, the Bible always remained the most important book to him.

Spurgeon was able to do what he did in the power of God's Holy Spirit because he followed his own advice – he met with God every morning before meeting with others, and he continued in communion with God throughout the day.

Charles Spurgeon suffered from gout, rheumatism,

and some depression, among other health problems. He often went to Menton, France, to recuperate and rest. He preached his final sermon at the Metropolitan Tabernacle on June 7, 1891, and died in France on January 31, 1892, at the age of fifty-seven. He was buried in Norwood Cemetery in London.

Charles Haddon Spurgeon lived a life devoted to God. His sermons and writings continue to influence Christians all over the world.

Similar Titles

The Soul Winner
by Charles H. Spurgeon

As an individual, you may ask, *How can I, an average person, do anything to reach the lost?* Or if a pastor, you may be discouraged and feel ineffective with your congregation, much less the world. Or perhaps you don't yet have a heart for the lost. Whatever your excuse, it's time to change. Overcome yourself and learn to make a difference in your church and the world around you. It's time to become an effective soul winner for Christ.

As Christians, our main business is to win souls. But, in Spurgeon's own words, "like shoeing-smiths, we need to know a great many things. Just as the smith must know about horses and how to make shoes for them, so we must know about souls and how to win them for Christ." Learn about souls, and how to win them, from one of the most acclaimed soul winners of all time.

Available where books are sold and free as an eBook

Jesus Came to Save Sinners
by Charles H. Spurgeon

This is a heart-level conversation with you, the reader. Every excuse, reason, and roadblock for not coming to Christ is examined and duly dealt with. If you think you may be too bad, or if perhaps you really are bad and you sin either openly or behind closed doors, you will discover that life in Christ is for you too. You can reject the message of salvation by faith, or you can choose to live a life of sin after professing faith in Christ, but you cannot change the truth as it is, either for yourself or for others. As such, it behooves you and your family to embrace truth, claim it for your own, and be genuinely set free for now and eternity. Come and embrace this free gift of God, and live a victorious life for Him.

Available where books are sold and free as an eBook

God's Promises
by Charles H. Spurgeon

The first part of this book is meant to be a sieve to separate the chaff from the wheat. Use it on your own soul. It may be the most profitable and beneficial work you have ever done. He who looked into his accounts and found that his business was losing money was saved from bankruptcy. This may happen also to you. If, however, you discover that your heavenly business is prospering, it will be a great comfort to you. You cannot lose by honestly searching your own heart.

The second part of this book examines God's promises to His children. The promises of God not only exceed all precedent, but they also exceed all imitation. No one has been able to compete with God in the language of liberality. The promises of God are as much above all other promises as the heavens are above the earth.

Available where books are sold and free as an eBook

Words of Counsel
by Charles H. Spurgeon

Is there any occupation as profitable or rewarding as that of winning souls for Christ? It is a desirable employment, and the threshold for entry into this profession is set at a level any Christian may achieve – you must only love the Lord God with all your heart, soul, and mind; and your fellow man as yourself. This work is for all genuine Christians, of all walks of life. This is for you, fellow Christian.

Be prepared to be inspired, challenged, and convicted. Be prepared to weep, for the Holy Spirit may touch you deeply as you consider your coworkers, your neighbors, the children you know, and how much the Lord cares for these individuals. But you will also be equipped. Charles Spurgeon knew something about winning souls, and he holds nothing back as he shares biblical wisdom and practical application regarding the incredible work the Lord wants to do through His people to reach the lost.

Available where books are sold and free as an eBook

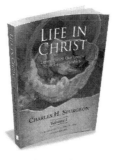

Life in Christ
by Charles H. Spurgeon

Men who were led by the hand or groped their way along the wall to reach Jesus were touched by his finger and went home without a guide, rejoicing that Jesus Christ had opened their eyes. Jesus is still able to perform such miracles. And, with the power of the Holy Spirit, his Word will be expounded and we'll watch for the signs to follow, expecting to see them at once. Why shouldn't those who read this be blessed with the light of heaven? This is my heart's inmost desire.

I can't put fine words together. I've never studied speech. In fact, my heart loathes the very thought of intentionally speaking with fine words when souls are in danger of eternal separation from God. No, I work to speak straight to your hearts and consciences, and if there is anyone with faith to receive, God will bless them with fresh revelation.

Available where books are sold and free as an eBook

Pilgrim's Progress
by John Bunyan

Often disguised as something that would help him, evil accompanies Christian on his journey to the Celestial City. As you walk with him, you'll begin to identify today's many religious pitfalls. These are presented by men such as Pliable, who turns back at the Slough of Despond; and Ignorance, who believes he's a true follower of Christ when he's really only trusting in himself. Each character represented in this allegory is intentionally and profoundly accurate in its depiction of what we see all around us, and unfortunately, what we too often see in ourselves. But while Christian is injured and nearly killed, he eventually prevails to the end. So can you.

Available where books are sold and free as an eBook

The Pursuit of God
by A.W. Tozer

To have found God and still to pursue Him is a paradox of love, scorned indeed by the too-easily-satisfied religious person, but justified in happy experience by the children of the burning heart. Saint Bernard of Clairvaux stated this holy paradox in a musical four-line poem that will be instantly understood by every worshipping soul:

> _We taste Thee, O Thou Living Bread,_
> _And long to feast upon Thee still:_
> _We drink of Thee, the Fountainhead_
> _And thirst our souls from Thee to fill._

Come near to the holy men and women of the past and you will soon feel the heat of their desire after God. Let A. W. Tozer's pursuit of God spur you also into a genuine hunger and thirst to truly know God.

Available where books are sold and free as an eBook

Made in the
USA
Monee, IL